T0270652

WHERE'S
YOUR BUFFALO?

WHERE'S YOUR BUFFALO?

A Recruiter's Guide to Getting the Career You Want, Earning What You're Worth, and Doing What You Love

Tom Johnston

PEAKPOINT
—— PRESS ——

Contents

This book is dedicated to my wife Amy,
the best placement I ever made.

Introduction

In a brightly lit church basement one winter evening, I looked out at dozens of adults who had come to my session seeking career advice. It was 2008, and the United States was reeling from a major downturn in the economy. For many of us, life seemed to have shut down. The fortunate among us were able to keep working, while many others suddenly found themselves unemployed, confused, and frightened.

My audience included many people with different needs. Some were unemployed and actively looking for a new opportunity. About half a dozen had good jobs but were unhappy or were afraid they'd lose their jobs because of the economic downturn. There were mothers trying to get back into the workforce after caring for their families, veterans back from military service looking for "civilian" job opportunities, young adults and recent college grads with no idea how to land a first "real" job, and older adults whose positions had suddenly disappeared. There were a few who were dreaming of launching their own business. I even had a young man who had recently been released from prison. What struck me was that even though the group was diverse in age, gender, background, and experience, they had one thing in common: no one had any idea how to find work that would make them happy and help get their lives back on track. At that moment I recognized how valuable my experience as an executive search consultant could be for each of these people and for many, many more like them. Years of connecting my clients who were looking to hire talented staff with the right people searching for great career opportunities showed me what matters most in this process. That insight led me to embark on another chapter in my own career journey.

If my story from 2008 sounds familiar, it's because the 2020 global COVID-19 pandemic upended millions of lives in very similar ways. As we emerge after three years of tremendous uncertainty, the work I began fifteen years ago is more relevant and valuable than ever. The same confusing employment future faced by those people in the church basement in 2008 exists today for workers at all stages of their careers.

So, how can I help? I've been a leader in the executive search industry for more than thirty years. My expertise in strategically identifying, recruiting, and placing top-notch candidates across every major industry sector and business function has earned me global recognition as the "Headhunter's Headhunter." What has given me the greatest satisfaction is using my ability to recognize, develop, and nurture every candidate's unique strengths and abilities. Teaching men and women to harvest their individual potential and compete for and win the roles they desire is what I do best.

Back in 2008, that group of people in the church basement showed me that by sharing my methodology as a recruiter, by teaching each of them to *think like a recruiter*, I could help each individual find their way forward to a better career and a better life. As a search consultant, I normally charge a fee equal to 30 percent of my candidates' first year's compensation. If I taught people how to evolve from being a reactive job seeker into a proactive job hunter, those who could not afford my fee would still be able to greatly improve their employment options. This was an aha moment. I realized I could help an even larger audience by creating a step-by-step program based on my proven talent search and placement methodology.

My initial offering was a collaborative ebook, *The Headhunter's Approach.*

Using the experience gained by working with hundreds of candidates since 1996, I have refined and greatly expanded the original concepts into *Where's Your Buffalo? A Recruiter's Guide to Getting the Career You Want, Earning What You're Worth, and Doing What*

You Love. This book fills the urgent need for an up-to-date, practical, realistic, and easily accessible approach to building and executing a lifetime career plan—in today's market.

The techniques I share with you throughout the book are goal driven, straightforward, measurable, and highly focused. You will learn how *to think and act like a professional executive recruiter.* The difference in mindset is dramatic. Instead of being a *reactive job seeker* (asking someone to please hire you), you'll become a *proactive job hunter* (searching for the ideal employer who will be lucky to hire you). And instead of bouncing randomly from job to job, the *Where's Your Buffalo?* program enables you to make clear decisions that will create a more direct path to reach your career target, or as I like to call it, your "Buffalo." (Chapter 1 will explain what I mean by "Buffalo.")

My *Where's Your Buffalo?* methodology teaches you how to:

- Better understand your skills and talents
- Articulate what is important to you in a job and why
- Identify industries that will support what is important to you
- Determine your target destination (we can adjust course as conditions change)
- Research and understand the companies that can provide you with a path
- Build a targeted network to help you along the way
- Learn how to hunt for the job you want

One of most important concepts you will learn is "competitive interviewing" to ensure you land a position in the career you want, where you want, while earning the compensation you desire. (To supplement the information and exercises you'll find in this book, training videos and short online courses are also available through MyHuntPath.com.)

My aim is to equip you with the techniques of highly successful executive search consultants, so that you can serve as your own professional job hunter.

Most people are unsure of their job security and are realizing that planning for what-ifs has become an everyday fact of life. Building a career is far from a "set it and forget it" type of process, whether you're a recent college graduate, a CEO, or somewhere in between. A successful career life transition involves thought, preparation, and planned actions. It requires reviewing one's background, goals, and experiences. It involves identifying significant accomplishments, values, capabilities, environmental/workplace/cultural preferences, and lifestyles. It's a process that is only successful when treated as a deep personal commitment with a significant investment of time and patience.

Finding a satisfying and rewarding career is daunting for everyone. And as my experience in the church basement brought home to me, many people do not know where to begin their journey. Now, more than ever, it is up to each of us to take charge of our careers. Making a solid plan built on honest self-assessment and market reality is the most important step.

The widespread disruption caused by the COVID-19 pandemic has dramatically altered the workplace. Opportunities for hybrid or remote work abound, employees in the current tight labor market have more negotiating power than before, and changes in society mean new opportunities for entrepreneurs and innovators. So, while uncertainty is always part of life, now is actually a great time to take control of your future and look for new opportunities. Keep in mind that this is a lifetime journey to help you find your next role, though you will be continually moving forward and looking for what new paths the future holds.

Success always starts with a clear vision of what you want, an understanding of what is possible, and the determination to take the necessary steps to get there. Over the course of my long career, I've seen the powerful, positive transformation that happens when good people find a great career-focused opportunity. My wish for you is that by applying all you will learn from the lessons and exercises on the following pages, you'll eventually reach your own "Buffalo" and enjoy the deep satisfaction that comes from work well done and a satisfying career.

CHAPTER 1

Finding Direction

There is a lot of advice out there about how to take control of your career. But from my perspective as a successful headhunter, most of it is completely useless.

Posting to job boards. Responding to online employment portals. Sending reams of résumés. Following your passion. Even if any of these methods actually land you a job, is it an opportunity that helps you advance in your career, or just something you do to earn a paycheck until you move on to the next job in a long string of unsatisfying, directionless employment?

This book will provide you with the tools and techniques to *stop chasing jobs and start building a fulfilling career.*

What's the difference between a job and a career? You work at a *job* to make money. You pursue a *career* to earn a living, sure, but also to find purpose, satisfaction, and even happiness. When you consider that you will most likely spend from forty to fifty years working, have as many as fourteen to eighteen different positions over your lifetime, and make a move to a new role every three or four years, wouldn't you feel more confident having a process and a plan?

I've used my decades of experience as an executive search consultant (what some people refer to as a recruiter or a headhunter) to craft this program organized to help you refine *your process* and define *your plan.* Taking the first step is up to you. If you're ready to begin shaping your future, your journey begins by deciding "Where's your Buffalo?" or "WYB."

The WYB Origin Story

A bit about me. I'm a sailor—not a great sailor, but sailing has been part of my identity since my teenage years. I like everything about sailing—the planning, the preparation, caring for the boat, the excitement of choosing a new destination. Being a competent sailor requires a variety of skills and abilities, but one of the first requirements when you set out is *knowing where you are going.* It might seem obvious, but a fair bit of careful research and advance planning has to happen before you untie the boat and set sail. You could of course just choose to sail around a lake in big circles, but that gets boring fast. Like most people, when I set out on a journey, I want to feel like I am moving in a positive direction, always getting closer to my intended target until I have the satisfaction of reaching the shore.

I live in Cleveland, Ohio, and whenever I can, I sail on Lake Erie. If you look on a map, you'll see that Cleveland is on the south shore, kind of in the middle. Buffalo, New York, is at the far eastern end of the lake. Toledo sits in the southwest corner, and Detroit is in the northeast corner. There are lots of places I could visit in between and detours I could take. But if I decide that Buffalo is my ultimate destination, I start by plotting the most direct course possible that will get me there. Seems pretty simple, right?

There are limitations to this process. I have to make the trip entirely on the water—no landing somewhere else and driving my car the rest of the way. I'm sailing on my own and have to rely on myself to manage the course. If I want to get there in one piece, first I have to be honest. Are my sailing skills up to the challenge? Or is it wishful thinking that I can get to Buffalo without a more experienced sailor by my side? This is not a question you want to fool yourself about, because the consequences could be serious.

There are numerous things I have to take into consideration as I develop my plan. How much time do I have for the journey? Do I have the right gear? Have I made sure the boat is ready, in excellent repair, and well supplied? Have I checked for a favorable weather forecast? I have to accept in advance that there will be conditions I can't control and some I can't possibly anticipate—sudden changes in the weather, the wind, or the current. What will I do if something doesn't go according to plan? Have I done everything I can to make sure my trip will be safe, successful, and enjoyable? If it is not going to be all of those things, why do I want to go?

Once I decide that I really, really want to get to Buffalo, I have defined my destination. I know once I'm there I'll feel like I've accomplished something worthwhile. I will feel proud and happy. I will know my time spent training and preparing for the trip, planning my route, and carefully executing my plan has been worthwhile. I may meet some unexpected hurdles along the way, but I know I'll be able to handle them and keep going until I reach the docks in Buffalo.

When I set out to write this book, my experience as a sailor provided me with a useful metaphor for approaching career choices and decisions. For me, sailing to Buffalo required skills similar to those needed to find rewarding work—the process takes discipline, skill, self-knowledge, dedication, resilience, and persistence. Everyone reading this book, from a college student to a senior executive, will have their own unique dreams, ambitions, and visions for their destination—their own Buffalo. Your Buffalo can and will evolve over time, based on your life. Sailing to Buffalo is an easy analogy to help you understand the process of coming up with and building a lifetime career management plan.

It starts with understanding who you are and what is most meaningful to you. So, when I ask, "Where's *your* Buffalo?" I'm urging you to describe what you hope your life will be—the kind of work you'll do, where you want to live, how much you will earn, and what other significant personal goals and life ambitions you want to pursue.

If you choose your career by starting with a clear understanding of how you hope to live your entire life—not just your nine-to-five work life—and undertake a realistic assessment of what it will take to achieve that vision, you're much more likely to get to your Buffalo.

Throughout this book, we'll look at numerous examples of real people I have helped at various stages of their career journey. Their experiences help highlight the way to making more informed choices, more practical plans, and more attainable goals. As an added bonus, at the end of each chapter, you'll also hear from a number of other professionals who have tips and insights to offer.

Get ready to go on a challenging and exciting trip. Together, we're going to plot a course to your Buffalo.

Lizzie Learns by Doing

Lizzie loved puppies and kittens—playing with them, feeding them, and cracking up at their funny antics. By the time she was in high school, she had set her sights on becoming a small animal vet.

Her family encouraged her to spend some time volunteering in a veterinary practice. What Lizzie discovered was profound. Instead of caring for playful dogs and cats, the pets she saw were often injured, seriously sick, or even terminally ill. Their owners were anxious, stressed, and deeply sad. Lizzie was seeing the reality of the profession, not the dreamy vision.

She still loved animals but knew she was not cut out to be a vet. During her college years, she found other internships and summer jobs that exposed her to more aspects of veterinary medicine including a position with a biotech startup doing animal health research. With each exploration, Lizzie was able to better define what felt like a realistic career goal. Because she started testing ideas while still in high school, what she learned about the profession and about herself helped her select the right college and pursue relevant coursework.

Lizzie's "Buffalo" was caring for animals. As she learned more about veterinary medicine and about herself, she pivoted—or in sailing language "tacked"—away from her original idea of becoming a small animal vet. Being open to other possibilities while still staying true to her goal of helping cats and dogs enabled her to find a career path with purpose—and start making progress toward her true "Buffalo."

In the spirit of total disclosure, Lizzie is one of my three children. I'm sharing her story (with her permission of course!) to show you how much I believe in the power of this process. I'm such a believer I even use it with my own children! Being thoughtful about what we want and what we cherish most has helped us as a family. It has guided our decisions about our children's education just as it has helped my wife and I make career pivots. I believe you will find, as we have, that you can return to the "Where's Your Buffalo?" method to enable you to make better career choices at key decision points throughout your life.

OMG, WYB?

Where do I even start? Ask anyone who makes something, and they'll tell you getting started is the hardest part. The blank page for a writer, the empty canvas for a painter, the stack of lumber for a furniture maker. They'll also tell you that how you start is the most important part. Getting it right takes time, skill, and hard work. It means facing uncertainty and taking chances. And believing in yourself.

Usually there's not only one "right" answer. And there will be things you learn along the way that continue to shape your choices and even change your direction if you are open and honest with yourself.

I tell you all this to help you get past the inevitable feeling of paralysis that sets in when someone asks you, "What do you want to do with your life?" It's a huge, scary question. Too big to take on with absolute confidence when there is so much you can't possibly know in advance.

What works for the thousands of people I have helped is to begin with a series of smaller questions that are easier to answer. Lots of answers to simpler questions adds up to a big, useful picture. I've found this same process to be equally successful for all sorts of people at various life stages. Young people still in high school or college. Young adults starting full-time employment. Women reentering the workforce after taking a break for family reasons. Men and women reentering civilian life after military service. Returning citizens who have been incarcerated. People at mid-career who are burnt out or disillusioned. Motivated workers who are looking to get to the next level in their careers. Older workers not yet ready to retire but uncertain how to stay engaged in a meaningful way.

My work has shown that each of the people in these very different life stages benefits from completing a baseline assessment. Though the questions vary a bit, the process is similar.

We start small to get big, valuable insights.

Executive Plans an Exit

Bob spent many years successfully climbing the corporate ladder. He'd reached the senior VP level in a Fortune 500 company where he enjoyed working. But as he looked ahead to what were likely to be his retirement years, he felt he had some ambitions left unexplored. He was at a crossroads. As we talked, Bob told me, "I could stay here, but I want something different."

Bob had a long-standing interest in ultra-high-level athletic competition. Although it was very different from his career, he had been thinking about what seemed to him to be a niche business opportunity—developing a line of nutrients and supplements for this elite group of athletes.

By working with me through my extensive set of questions (see chapter 2), Bob came to realize how he might make his dream real. He could see a way to get to his new "Buffalo" with confidence.

Late in his career, but in the time that was right for him, he left his corporate position to launch the company he'd dreamt of. Instead of sliding into retirement, Bob is now enthusiastically, happily living in Colorado where he runs a successful nutritional company for competitive ultra-athletes.

Start Your Self-assessment

Close your eyes, then let yourself relax and dream big. Don't worry about whether your ideas seem realistic at this point. When you wake up in three years . . .

- What does your life look like?
- Where are you living?
- How much money are you making?
- How do you spend your day?
- How does that feel?

If you can already answer these questions without much hesitation, you're ready to move on to your road map and develop a "Business Plan for Life" (see chapter 2). But for most of us, the best we can do is to come up with partial answers or even more questions. That's why I suggest starting with a slightly more detailed baseline assessment.

You'll want to write down your answers, probably in pencil so you can erase and change your mind! These answers are just for you, so be as honest as you can. We're asking about your current situation in work and life, about your past experiences that have brought you to this point, and about your readiness to do whatever it takes to make significant changes. There's no need to impress anyone else or say what you think someone else wants to hear. This is 100 percent about what you believe to be true about you.

It's All About You

1. Briefly describe your current situation. For example, "I'm a junior in college," "I'm stuck in a dead-end job," "I made some missteps and want to get back on track," "I need to make more money," or however you see where you are right now.
2. Outline your current role. How did you get this job? What do you like most about it? What don't you like and want to change?
3. What is the *biggest* challenge facing you right now? Are you holding yourself back or is there something else making change difficult?
4. What are your best talents and skills?
5. What do you wish you could do more of or were better at?
6. What was your favorite job? What did you like most about it? What parts did you not like?
7. If you could live anywhere, where would it be?
8. Are you ready to face some hard decisions with real consequences?
9. Are you willing to make some trade-offs to get on a more rewarding career path? Or does it have to be "all or nothing?"
10. Do you think your goals and ambitions are realistic? Why or why not?

That was probably hard, even more difficult if you are currently out of work. This process is hard because we don't get much practice asking ourselves these questions, and we aren't encouraged early in our lives to ask them. For too long, the advice has been to land a good job with a solid company and stay there for life. Or worse yet, the wishful thinking that urges you to "follow your passion and the money will follow."

The reality is much starker. Just about nobody in the workforce today will retire with a pension after thirty years at one company. And how exactly does "passion" turn into "profit?"

Tough as it may seem, the current employment market is also super encouraging. Coming out of the massive disruptions caused by the COVID-19 pandemic, the workplace has become far more flexible, making the freedom of hybrid work a new reality for many. Much of the negotiating power has shifted from employers to employees because of labor shortages, and many new opportunities have opened up for gig workers, solo entrepreneurs, and small businesses.

It's always challenging to figure out your future and make a plan to get there, but in so many ways, this is the ideal time for you to do just that. In chapter 2, you'll answer many more probing questions as you work on describing your Buffalo. Honestly and thoughtfully completing these exercises will give you the initial information you need to begin mapping a realistic way forward.

Dreaming, Planning, and Reality Checking

Consider chapter 1 the warm-up for the work you are about to tackle. You've answered, or at least tried to answer, some of the big questions about your life and career. Over the next several pages, I'll ask you to be much more specific. Throughout this chapter, my goal is to help you begin to build some important, defining details around your Buffalo.

I call this process writing your **Business Plan for Life**. Yes, that sounds daunting. And it would be if I expected you to just start writing. But after helping thousands of opportunity seekers (a.k.a. job hunters) move closer to or arrive at their Buffalo, I've developed the following set of assessments to guide you, along with a useful rating system for determining what matters most to you.

Taken together, you'll have a quantitative and qualitative method for evaluating what you value the most. Then you can use your new insights to evaluate how each new option compares to your current situation and how it may either advance or derail your progress on the way to your Buffalo.

But the Where's Your Buffalo? (WYB) process takes you even further. It's not enough to have dreams. You need to get real. About your skills and experience. About your willingness to invest time and money in advanced training (if getting closer to your Buffalo requires it).

About your desire to ultimately launch your own business. And once you've done that self-assessment, I'll show you how to go deeper into market research to uncover where your next realistic opportunities can be found.

The WYB system works no matter where you are in your career: starting out, stalled at the midpoint, thinking about "tacking" to a new career, reentering the workforce as a free agent, starting your own enterprise, or planning a transition to or after retirement. Being able to use this same approach repeatedly to help you choose your path at various career stages is how it became known as a Business Plan *for Life*.

Let's get started with a story, perhaps one you've heard before.

What Are Your Priorities?

The late author and motivational speaker Stephen Covey used a powerful metaphor for making sense of the many life decisions we face. He called it the "Big Rocks" theory (you can find his version on YouTube). In short, Covey wants you to picture a container like a bucket or a big jar. Place in that jar as many big rocks as you can. Is the container full?

What happens if you pour some gravel over the rocks? Is it full now? How about trying to pour some sand over the gravel? Now add some water.

The point Covey is making is to *always start with the "big rocks" because these are the things that really matter.* Once the big rocks are in place, there is still room for more. But if you reverse the process, start with water and try to finagle your way through sand and gravel, there will *never* be room for the big rocks, the things you care most about that make your life richer and more rewarding every day.

In my Business Plan for Life model, the "big rocks" are the essentials that must be considered when planning your career path or making a career change. These are the deciding factors that, when they are all or mostly in place, will cause you to wake up happy in work and life most of the time! Your descriptions for each of these aspects of life and work provide signposts pointing to your Buffalo.

Get ready to describe your ideals for:

1. location—where do you want to be?
2. income goal or potential to reach that goal (short- and long-term)
3. lifestyle
4. professional/personal growth
5. work culture/environment

1. Location

It used to be that for many of us this was the single biggest consideration. Where do I have to live in order to do this job? How long is my commute going to be? What is the cost of living? Can I afford to buy a house there? Is there a good school system for my kids?

But in our post-pandemic work world where hybrid or fully remote work is possible for many types of positions, more options have become available to you.

What matters to you when it comes to location? Is it being near your family and loved ones? Year-round weather conditions? Access to cultural or athletic activities? Ease of travel to other parts of the country or world? Are there places that are "deal-breakers" where you would never consider living? Is your family or significant other willing to relocate?

Location, Location, Location

It used to be said that these were the three most important elements of a successful business. But since the dawn of online commerce, the Internet has enabled many businesses to thrive without being limited to brick and mortar locations. However, for many entrepreneurs, especially in service industries, location remains an important factor.

Tessa, a client of mine, was a young woman about to graduate from a culinary school in New England. Her ambition was to open her own restaurant, and she had settled on Providence, Rhode Island, for her location. Although Tessa was originally from Cleveland, she had fallen in love with Providence and wanted to be able to put down roots there. She came to me for advice about how to make her dream of owning a restaurant come true.

"How many people do you know in Providence?" I asked her.

"None," she replied.

"On opening night, how many people will come to support your café because they want you to succeed?"

"Probably none," she answered sadly.

"If you opened a café in Cleveland, how many people would show up that first night because they wanted to support you?" I asked.

Tessa smiled. "Probably hundreds, even more than I could possibly feed!"

Cleveland suddenly looked like a much better location for her dream restaurant.

Dream locations, just like any dreams, have to be weighed against reality. Starting a business is really hard work. The failure rate is soberingly high. If ownership is your dream, being realistic can help to eliminate early roadblocks and help position you for success.

This also applies to a traditional career move. If you really want to build your life and career in New York City, don't waste your time looking for opportunities in Los Angeles, Houston, or Anchorage.

On a scale of 1 to 10, with 10 being the most important to you, rate how important living/working in a specific location is to you: _____

2. Income Potential

The amount of money needed to maintain your current lifestyle will vary based on where you are in your life. Are you only supporting yourself? Are you the sole or primary breadwinner for your family? How would earning more money change your daily quality of life? How would earning more enable you to reach your goals? Consider the short- and long-term potential of each opportunity you are considering, as well as how it may position you for future earnings. You also must consider what you are willing to give up.

It's helpful to keep in mind that, while we all need money, money may not be as important as career growth, opportunity, or flexibility—what you do every day is more important. Many studies have shown that beyond a certain earning level, money really does not buy happiness. Not loving what you do every day really impacts how you feel about yourself and can spill over into lessening the quality of your family's life and your participation in your community.

As you think about your desired income, consider how much earnings and earnings potential mean to your overall contentment and satisfaction.

No Wrong Answers

A recent college graduate named Todd came to me seeking advice about his career path. My father taught me to listen first and speak last, so I began my conversation with this young man by asking what things were important to him. When I asked about income goals, he hesitated. "If I tell you my honest answer," Todd said, "you won't take me seriously."

With an encouraging smile, I replied, "Try me."

"I want to make $10 million a year," he said, and waited for my reaction.

"Well," I said, "if that's your goal, we can start by eliminating many careers that will never offer that level of compensation. Then we can begin to focus on paths with the earnings potential you want."

We started by exploring sales roles and looking at entrepreneurial options most likely to eventually enable Todd to reach his income target.

My point is that there is no right answer to this or any of these assessment questions. What's right for you is what matters. You're ultimately the only judge of the "rightness" of your answer to the income question. Does it make you feel your time and talents are well used and fairly compensated in a realistic context?

On a scale of 1 to 10, how important is the level of income a position offers? _____

3. Lifestyle

Dream for a moment that you won the lottery. What would you do if you never had to worry about money? Would you be working, traveling, pursuing a passion, or spending more time with your family? What is the level of importance of having a life outside of work? What work/life balance will make you happy? For most people, it's not about money. It's about finding something they truly love and spending their days doing just that.

More than ever, millennials and Gen Z adults consider lifestyle to be a very important aspect when considering opportunities. Flexibility? More personal control over your time? Running your own business might put you more in control, while working for someone can limit that freedom.

Another key element that is becoming more and more important is feeling that what we do has value beyond a paycheck—that we may even have a purpose or mission. A trend especially prevalent among younger workers is a desire to find careers that are positive and impactful.

Taking money off the table, what do you want to do? The next step is to make sure that your career plan matches your goals. If we put money back into the equation, will your work choices enable you to support your lifestyle choices?

Barrels of Fun

Rob was a successful senior executive who had grown tired of the banking industry. He came to me looking for a new position, though he really didn't see any options outside of banking. "Well, Rob, when you're not working, what do you enjoy doing?" I began. Rob enthusiastically described how he spent his weekends making furniture. He'd converted his garage to a semi-professional woodworking studio. He drove around to various suppliers to acquire used bourbon barrels. Then he worked out designs for all sorts of furniture and fabricated each unique piece from the repurposed wood. Rob was able to sell every item of furniture he made at a significant price, so his hobby was self-sustaining. Plus, he was as happy as could be in his workshop.

"Could you make a business out of your hobby?" I asked.

"Gee, I never even thought about that. I'm going to do some research. I'll put some numbers together and let's talk again," Rob said.

The next time we met, Rob proudly showed me the business plan he'd carefully put together for a furniture business. He'd done his research and his numbers were solid. His excitement was obvious too. Together we crafted a transition plan for him to slowly build and test the new business before exiting his banking job. His family was 100 percent behind the plan. Rob used his business skills to make his passion his new career.

On a scale of 1 to 10, rate how important a particular lifestyle is to you: _____

4. Professional/Personal Growth

Where do you want to be in five years? If you have a burning desire to build your own business, what options will help you achieve that goal? If one option requires you to dig ditches all day, it may not be a great job with great income—but will it bring you closer to your goal?

Ideally, how you spend your day should be rewarding, or at least put you on a path toward higher accomplishments with more personal and professional satisfaction.

One Track Career

Meredith grew up in a family that placed a very high value on education. Her mom and dad were both teachers who loved their jobs, their work schedules with summers off, and the lifestyle their careers made possible for their family. Although it was never explicitly said, everyone assumed Meredith would follow in her parents' footsteps and become a teacher.

That's exactly what happened. For several years Meredith enjoyed teaching elementary school children. She and her husband bought a lovely home where they were raising their two children. The family owned two nice cars, took relaxing summer vacations, and generally were enjoying their lives together. But over time, Meredith began to feel something was missing from her career.

The stress of dealing with the emotional and physical needs of her young students started to wear her down and the politics and drama in the teacher's lounge was stifling. By the weekend she felt too tired to do much more than keep up with household chores. Meredith began to wonder if teaching was not her ultimate career. But she had no idea how to even begin looking for alternatives.

One day a mutual friend introduced Meredith and me. We set up a coffee meeting to get acquainted. When I asked her about her career, she shared her increasing frustration with teaching and her confusion about what else she could possibly do. She was afraid that her unhappiness would begin to affect her interactions with students and her family. She did not want to become a teacher who was "phoning it in." But since she had never considered any other career besides teaching, she didn't have a clue what else might be possible.

It took more than one coffee conversation, but Meredith worked with me to identify a new career path. She was highly motivated, willing to commit to the time and expense of re-training and accepting of the fact that making a change would be a gradual process requiring both financial preparation and the support of her family.

Her excitement about new career opportunities gave her the energy she needed to make the transition. She is now a very successful executive recruiter, earning a higher salary than her teaching position, but even more importantly, feeling challenged and rewarded by her work life. Meredith told me, "I feel like I discovered a whole new side of myself with talents and abilities I never knew I had. The future looks very exciting to me now."

On a scale of 1 to 10, rate how important opportunities for professional/personal growth are: _____

5. Work Culture/Environment

This is something that people too rarely consider. Having to work all day with someone you do not like or respect can be very difficult. Whenever possible, spend some real time evaluating each opportunity and the people you will spend the vast majority of your time with. What does the workplace look and feel like? Consider not just how people are dressed, but how they interact with one another. How are you treated as a visitor or applicant? What values does the company promote? Are these just slogans or are they meaningful commitments? Are the company values in line with your own?

Culture Matters

Recently I heard from a senior executive who had just made what she thought would be an exciting career move to an international organization. Instead, within a few weeks of making the transition, Suzanne experienced what she described as a "toxic" work environment. Her supervisor, the same person who had hired her, ignored or even belittled her ideas. Her coworkers were afraid to do anything but go along with the boss's unpredictable and disruptive management style. The advice of her coworkers was to "keep your head down." That was the way they avoided being fired. Suzanne had left a satisfying, high-profile job to join this international firm, but the negative culture proved to be too powerful to overcome. She quit after six miserable weeks and went back on the job market.

On a scale of 1 to 10, how important is the culture/environment of a workplace to you? _____

What's the Score?

Congratulations! If you've been able to rate the importance of each of these key elements of a balanced and happy work life, you've done some serious self-evaluation. But don't worry. You can change your answers at any time. The fact is, as we move through life, the things that matter most to us often change. Early on in your career, a work culture/environment might mean a great deal to you. Years later, once you have an established network and perhaps a rich life outside of work, this may carry less weight. Similarly, the importance of income potential may decrease later in your career if you've been fortunate enough to save for a comfortable retirement.

But for now, let's enter your current rankings as the baseline for helping you to begin to define your Buffalo. The chart below will enable you to make side-by-side comparisons of what you want versus what you currently have.

Please enter the five ratings you just completed in the column labeled "Importance to Me."

	Importance to Me	Current Position	New Option #1	New Option #2
Location				
Income/Potential				
Lifestyle				
Professional/ Personal Growth				
Work Culture/ Environment				
Other				
Other				
Total score				

(A more detailed chart with some additional categories is available online at MyHuntPath.com. The online version can be saved, then easily modified or replaced each time you revisit your Business Plan for Life or want to evaluate a new opportunity.)

How Does Your Current Situation Measure Up?

Next you'll find a series of Yes or No questions. Answering these honestly will help you determine how you value your current situation. The following questions take into account the five key categories previously discussed. This section asks you to think critically about your current role. Just jot down a "yes" or "no" for each question.

1. *Do I have enough time to spend with my family and friends?*
2. *Do I have enough time to do the things I truly enjoy?*
3. *Am I active in social activities outside of work?*
4. *Do I have a good work/life balance?*
5. *Do I have a solid support system?*

6. *Do I have any flexibility in my daily schedule?*
7. *Am I happy with my current geographical location?*
8. *Is relocation an option at this point in my life?*
9. *Do I have the ability to work from wherever I want?*
10. *Can I advance in my career if I stay where I am?*
11. *Do I enjoy the climate where I live?*
12. *Is living close to family important?*
13. *Am I happy with my current income?*
14. *Do I make what I feel I am worth?*
15. *Do I have financial freedom with my current income?*
16. *Can I increase my income if I stay with my current employer?*
17. *Have I been promised a raise in the past year?*
18. *Did I receive that raise?*
19. *Does the idea of starting a company excite me?*
20. *Do I enjoy taking on new challenges?*
21. *Do I shy away from financially risky situations?*
22. *Am I afraid of failure?*
23. *Am I passionate about what I do at work?*
24. *Do I get to utilize my skill set as much as I would like?*
25. *Do I still feel like I have a lot to learn?*
26. *Do I like my current working environment?*
27. *Am I in line for a promotion in the next year?*
28. *Is there growth in my current industry?*
29. *Is there a great training/mentoring program at my current position?*
30. *Are my ideas taken into consideration at work?*

Once you've run through these questions, use your answers to help you rate how you view your current position. Go back to the previous chart and record your ratings for your present situation in the second column. *Remember, we are using a rating system in which 10 is the highest value, while 1 is the least valuable.*

Now add up the numbers in each column to get your total score for each category.

Here's an example of how the chart reveals insights about the possible gap between what you have and what you want. In this scenario, the low score assigned to the current position indicates that it may be time for a change! This person is not currently near or getting any closer to her Buffalo.

	Importance to Me	Current Position	New Option #1	New Option #2
Location	9	5		
Income Potential	8	7		
Lifestyle	10	8		
Professional/ Personal Growth	7	2		
Work Culture/ Environment	8	4		
Other (Job security)	6	5		
Other				
Total score	48	31		

Feel free to add rows or columns to capture any additional factors that are meaningful to you. The additional columns allow you to evaluate new choices compared to what is most important to you and in contrast to your current situation. And keep in mind you can find a more detailed and customizable chart online at MyHuntPath.com.

Your Here and Now

The rating scale you've completed for your Business Plan for Life shows what you value most. Understanding what is likely to give you the most satisfaction in life and work enables you to make better decisions. Not having a value scale often means randomly wandering along without direction or goals. Because you've done some honest and thoughtful work, your Buffalo is beginning to take shape.

To get to your Buffalo, you need to know where (and what) it is. But you also have to understand where you are starting from. Psychologists have come to realize that human beings are most likely to be able to bring about significant change *when they perceive a gap between where they are and where they want to be.*

This next set of assessments will help you evaluate your current situation by capturing important aspects of your:

- work history
- education, training, and qualifications
- positive workplace dynamics

The information you gather here creates a baseline from which you'll be better able to identify and capitalize on the right future opportunities.

Work History

Please do not refer to or simply copy your existing résumé. This task is intended to provide you with an opportunity to gain a current and fresh perspective on your work life and career. All details regarding positions or jobs—full- or part-time—including volunteer activities are important in this exercise.

Describe the specific accomplishments that are important to you, regardless of what the outside world views as important.

Example: Directed the management of six lead engineers, twenty technicians, and three administrative staff in the development of automotive prototypes.

Please feel free to list all positions that have been meaningful in your life so far.

Organization/Company:
Title:
Start date:
End date:

Duties and Responsibilities included:
Accomplishments I am most proud of:

Organization/Company:
Title:
Start date:
End date:
Duties and Responsibilities included:
Accomplishments I am most proud of:

Organization/Company:
Title:
Start date:
End date:
Duties and Responsibilities included:
Accomplishments I am most proud of:

Organization/Company:
Title:
Start date:
End date:
Duties and Responsibilities included:
Accomplishments I am most proud of:

Organization/Company:
Title:
Start date:
End date:
Duties and Responsibilities included:
Accomplishments I am most proud of:

Organization/Company:
Title:
Start date:

End date:
Duties and Responsibilities included:
Accomplishments I am most proud of:

Organization/Company:
Title:
Start date:
End date:
Duties and Responsibilities included:
Accomplishments I am most proud of:

Education/Training/Qualifications

By completing this section, you will have the opportunity to identify what your previous education and experiences enable you to do. It
can show you areas of your greatest strength while indicating areas that
may benefit from additional effort or investment.

Degree School/University/College
Major(s) Year(s)

Additional Education and Training. Please list any seminars, special
training workshops, or courses you have attended.
Name of Course/Workshop
Licensure/Certification
Title Type/State Year(s)

Military Service
Branch Rank Year Special Training

Formal, informal, self-study efforts, corporate seminars, and/or related
levels of activity or experience.

Civic, professional organizations or memberships you currently or formerly belong to.
Please provide dates and mention any offices held.

Applicable published/unpublished materials, presentations, patents, and/or honors/awards.

Workplace Dynamics

In this section you can reflect on what types of activities and events motivate, gratify, or frustrate you. Seeing a pattern here or calling out specific examples can help you recognize the *kind of work* and the *type of workplace* that is most likely to bring you satisfaction.

Sweet Spots

What was your best day at work in the last three months?
What were you doing?
Who were you doing it with?
Why did you enjoy it so much?

Bummers

What was your worst day at work in the last three months?
What were you doing?
Who were you doing it with?
Why was it so unpleasant?

Motivators

Think of the best relationship you ever had with a manager.
What made it work so well?
What was the most meaningful praise or recognition you ever received?
What made it so good?

Growth

When in your career do you think you were learning the most?
What made it possible for you to learn then?
What is the best way for you to learn now?

Who Besides You?

Relax, stand up, and stretch. Grab a beverage or a snack, and get comfortable. You've earned a break after answering all those questions. Seriously!

As my father taught me, I always start my advice sessions by asking questions and then by really listening to what people say. Everyone has a different way of figuring out and defining their goals, then setting their strategies to reach them. For me it is never about "my way or the highway." The questions WYB poses are meant to start you on a journey of discovery. My personal and professional experience has shown me time and time again that you will *always* benefit from talking to other people you like and trust. Especially when they have knowledge and experience you lack.

While you work through all the questions and assessments this book offers, I encourage you to *invite a trusted partner, family member, friend, or peer to act as your sounding board.* Someone you know and feel comfortable with who also knows and understands you. Someone you can be totally honest with and who will be honest with you. It is certainly true that having to explain something to someone else in ways they can completely understand helps us sharpen and deepen our own understanding. Instead of saying, "I want a good job that I love," the result should be a clear, concise elevator pitch that enables you to effectively communicate in detail *exactly what your Buffalo is.*

I want to share another pair of stories, this time about how two very different people used a deep understanding of their past to shine a bright light on a future more rewarding than they thought possible. One thing to notice in each of these stories is the importance of involving other people in your discovery process. In my work helping people find their Buffalo, attentive conversation and deep listening are without a doubt the most powerful tools in the process. Let's see how getting another person's perspective changed the future for Franklin and Devin.

Aiming Higher

Over the years I have had the opportunity to bring the MyHuntPath.com program to various inmate populations in Northeast Ohio. That's how I met Franklin. After serving eight years for auto theft and drug offenses, he was soon to be released. His mother and extended family lived in Cleveland, so his plan was to move there. While incarcerated, Franklin had become certified as a welder. He told me his goal was to find a welding job in Cleveland.

That might have been a fine job, but it wasn't going to be much of a career. And welding two pieces of metal together didn't require the special skills and abilities Franklin already had. He'd run a drug business and an auto theft ring, managed employees, and made significant profits. He was a natural salesman, a capable manager, and an entrepreneur. When I described him in these terms he looked shocked. "Tom," he said, "no one has ever told me that what I did before going to prison was a good thing."

"Don't misunderstand me, Franklin, what you did wasn't good, but you were good at it," I told him. "I'm saying use those skills legitimately. Find a job that can become a career using your sales and management talents."

Instead of settling for a welder job, Franklin landed a sales and marketing position for a construction company. Higher pay, more potential for advancement, and a new, very positive self-image put him on a path to rebuilding his life as a respected member of his family and community. His attitude about himself and his future completely changed from fear, regret, and shame to hope.

It Takes Two

The *Where's Your Buffalo?* program starts by encouraging you to dream and think big about what will bring you the most happiness and satisfaction. Sometimes we can get everything we want. But more often, trade-offs and compromises are required. Especially when family is involved.

Devin was an IT whiz kid who had no trouble landing a well-paying job with a corporate employer. His tech position gave him regular hours, a reliable paycheck, and valuable benefits for himself and his wife. But it didn't satisfy his creative side. What gave Devin the greatest satisfaction was designing and applying custom tattoos.

He had experience and talent, and he loved the tattoo work. Devin roughed out his Business Plan for Life to set up his own tattoo business. He thought with some sacrifices he could make it work. It meant less income at least for a few years, working some nights and weekends, and dealing with the uncertainties of being self-employed. Still, he was willing to give it a try and leave his corporate gig behind.

His wife had other ideas. In her Business Plan for Life, Devin's corporate income and benefits provided the security she felt they needed to start a family. She didn't want to squash his dreams, but she didn't want to give up on hers either. So, where did they go from here?

By talking through each other's hopes and values, the couple was able to make a plan *together*. Devin would keep his IT job, but he'd have nights and weekends to take on a few high-end clients able to afford custom tattoos. Instead of having his own studio, Devin arranged to use a well-respected tattoo parlor nearby. The tattoo parlor owner was happy to showcase Devin's talents and Devin was spared the hassle and expense of starting his own shop. After a year of "compromise," the couple was very pleased with their blended Business Plan for Life. Soon afterwards, their baby girl was born.

How Your Ideas Become a Plan

By working through these assessments and self-evaluations, you've taken an honest look at who you are, what you have, and what you want—at least in general terms. You recognize what is important to you and what special traits and knowledge you have to offer. The next big phase in following my recruiter's methodology is to begin turning that information into a plan.

Even in the most sophisticated corporations, senior executives realize that there is no such thing as a five-year or ten-year plan set in stone. There are too many forces beyond our control or things that are simply unknowable about the future. Instead of having a step-by-step long-term plan, they form a road map based on their overall strategy and their competencies and capabilities—what they want to do and are capable of doing. That might sound too difficult to do on your own but it is what I mean by your Business Plan for Life. If you start with a clear idea of what you think you would ultimately like to be doing, along with an honest appraisal of what it takes to get there, what you already have, and what you may need to acquire, you have the elements in place to make each decision as it arises.

No plan has value unless there is solid research behind it. That might seem scary and impossible, but believe me, in the age of the Internet, the type of basic research this requires is only a few keystrokes away.

If you and I were talking, I'd ask you to tell me what industry interests you. You might say "the manufacturing industry, because I really like making things and I am good at it." That's a start, but we have to go deeper. What kinds of things do you enjoy making? What materials are you used to working with? At what scale or production volume do you envision working? Studio, workshop, vast high-volume production facility? In other words, "manufacturing" is way too broad a category.

Suppose you enjoy making clothing, working with wool, and prefer creating one-of-a-kind pieces for luxury buyers. Opportunities for that kind of work are going to be far different from someone who also wants to make garments out of wool but for a mass consumer audience across a high-volume global market.

To begin making your plan, be as specific as you can about what industry *niche* appeals to you.

Not long ago, I worked with a recent college graduate who wanted to be in banking. As we talked, he shared that he was really only interested in commercial lending; he wanted a firm with offices across the country, and he wanted to start his career in California. Our next step became clear. We googled commercial lenders with national offices, then checked that list for those companies with locations in California.

This is when your dreams and hopes start to become real through a process I call "validation": exploring specific roles, opportunities, and the companies who may be able to offer what you hope to find.

Validation, though, applies not just to potential companies but also to your overall qualifications. Recruiters refer to this as the **ABCs** of early stage planning. When you're considering career options, you have to evaluate yourself in these three areas.

A = ability. Do you have the necessary skills and capabilities that will enable you to fulfill the job requirements?

B = background. Does your level of education and/or training match the standards for this career?

C = commitment. If you don't have everything it takes to do this job now, are you willing and able to commit to the time, expense, effort, and sustained dedication—in some cases, years—it will take to qualify you? When my daughter Lizzie expressed interest in becoming a veterinarian, I told her it would mean at least four to six more years of school beyond her undergraduate degree. "I'm okay with that," she replied, and at least so far, she is sticking with her plan.

On the other hand, I once asked a recent high school graduate if he wanted to consider a career in health care. He emphatically stated that he really did not want to be a doctor because he didn't want to spend so much time and money fulfilling the education requirements. "That's not the only option for a health-care career," I suggested. Then I showed him a list of hundreds of health-care careers that don't require a medical school degree. Suddenly, he had many more realistic options to consider.

None of us can know the future, but if at the very outset, you honestly admit you don't have all of the ABCs, my advice is to go back to your self-assessment. Revisit these insights to help you find another more promising and attainable career path. At best, it's a waste of your time and talent to chase after something impossibly far out of reach, although that decision should be made by you (with help from those closest to you) and not by what the rest of the world thinks. If at age sixty-five, you want to finish your college degree and go on to earn a PhD in biology, that's your choice. Go for it if you truly have the ABCs and support system to pursue your dream.

What Role (Job) is Right for Me?

Identifying what segment of an industry you want to work in is one important step in making your Business Plan for Life. But within any industry segment, there are countless functions, roles, and possibilities. This is where the Work Experience and Workplace Dynamics self-assessments you've completed become valuable.

Look back at the tasks and accomplishments that have given you the most satisfaction in the past. What types of assignments or processes irritate, frustrate, or bore you? If you know, for example, that the sight of an Excel spreadsheet fills you with dread, you'll want to avoid any role that regularly requires quantitative data capture and analysis. If, on the other hand, your idea of a great day is data entry and reconciliation, you'll want to start with positions that prioritize these functions.

While we are all capable of learning new skills, it is harder if not impossible to change our preferences for a type of work. For introverts, sales jobs or customer relations positions are probably not the best fit. For extroverts who are energized by interactions with others, solo research roles or independent assignments are not likely to fill a need for connection. No one knows your preferences better than you do. So, as you're considering new positions, start with those that offer familiarity and assurance rather than choosing a big "stretch" goal far outside the comfort zone of your personality.

I want to take a minute to talk about the concept of sales. Many people, when asked about a sales role, instantly think of bad salespeople. The car salesman who tried to sell you a junker. The insurance person pressuring you into upping your coverage. When you are trying to advance your career, you must practice and improve your ability to sell yourself, your ideas, your wants, and your goals. A great salesperson doesn't push unnecessary stuff onto unsuspecting customers. A great salesperson solves problems.

As a young person, I never thought of myself as a salesman or felt I should pursue a career in sales. But at some point, I learned that salespeople usually get paid based on performance. I realized that I could earn much more than most people because I really did enjoy helping people by solving their problems. In my role as an executive recruiter, I sell my service offerings to clients and present career changing opportunities to candidates. Actually, I never "sell" anything, I just bring the right people together to help them solve their own problems. One person needs to hire someone to fill a key role. The other person is looking for meaningful employment that meets their goals and wants. My point here is not to rule out sales as a career. When practiced responsibly and creatively, it can be a very rewarding career option for those willing to become excellent problem-solvers.

That said, you'll want to approach a new opportunity by building on what you already know, are able to do competently, and believe will provide you with job satisfaction. In the language of recruiters, you are using your *functional strengths* based on your work history, personal interests, education and qualifications, skills, self-description, and ideal work environment to help determine which direction your career should take.

Especially for young people starting out, or perhaps for those who have been out of the employment market for some time, the positions possible in various careers are a mystery. The fact is, most of us are limited in our thinking about what's possible by what we have personally seen or experienced. It's no surprise that so many people follow in their parents' footsteps when it comes to choosing a career—they know what the work is like and what it takes to be successful. For many people, choosing the same career their parents pursued works out just fine. But for others like Meredith, whose story we read about in One Track Career, the satisfaction can be short-lived.

Opening up the possibilities begins by looking around you. Who do you know or who have you encountered whose work seems appealing to you? Young adults may have limited exposure to many professionals, but your parents, extended family members, neighbors, and business-people in your community may be able to provide additional resources. How about professionals you hear about through the media? Who has a career that looks attractive to you and at least appears to be deeply satisfying to them?

Once again, the Internet is your friend because it is very easy to research the earnings potential and professional requirements for virtu-ally every position in any industry. Start there, but if you find something that looks as if it meets your aspirations, continue your investigation by finding out what the work is really like. The most important thing I can say is to not stress about this. Talk to people to get their insights. This is a lifelong process with no right or wrong answers. It's a journey, so let yourself enjoy it!

I always advise people to get "insider information," and by that I mean learning as much as they can about their target industry. This is especially valuable for those considering a change of industry, and certainly for young adults or others without much previous work expe-rience. Start by talking to people who do this type of work. Ask them to connect for a coffee. Ask to shadow them by spending some time observing them at work. Volunteer your skills to enable you to spend time in their workplace. Take an internship, paid or unpaid, to get closer to the work. If you have something to offer, even if it is just enthusiasm and a willingness to learn, many people will be willing to invite you to intern with them—especially if you provide free labor. You may chafe at not being paid, but I tell people to think of it as a *low-cost investment* that is likely to have a *very high return*. In exchange for a few days or weeks of your time, you can gain insights into whether this is the career and company for you, or not. Plus, in the process you can be building your network of professionals who now know you and may be your future sponsors or supporters.

The image of the career and the reality of the work may be very, very different, which is something a client of mine learned in time to save him from making a costly misstep.

One Big Dinner Party

After building and selling a lucrative exercise equipment business, Terrence ("T" to his friends) had money in the bank and the freedom to take some time to consider what he wanted to do next. T told me he always thought he'd like to own a restaurant. He and his friends had a favorite spot for drinks and dinner, and they always enjoyed spending a relaxing evening there. After selling his business, T missed the daily interactions with customers and thought he'd find satisfaction meeting and greeting people in his own restaurant.

T had never worked in a restaurant, but had a buddy in the business who offered to bring him on as a waiter. He did well as a waiter and soon moved up to be the dining room manager. At our follow-up meeting, T told me about his promotion, but what he said next surprised me. "Tom, I'm good at this, but I don't want to do it. I'm working long hours, I never see my wife and kids, and even when I'm not at work, I worry about it all the time. I thought owning a restaurant would mean standing by the front door and greeting happy customers, but that's not the reality. It is way harder than I thought it was going to be."

What T learned by investing his time was that he should not invest his money and his life in a restaurant career. What he experienced as a customer was not at all what it was like to be a restaurateur responsible for creating a wonderful customer experience night after night. T was sorry to see his dream fade, but relieved that he had sidestepped what would have been a big, expensive mistake.

Employee, Free Agent, or Owner

We have more choices about the way we want to work in the post-pandemic landscape than ever before. As you consider the type of work you want to do in the industry niche of your choosing, think about the way you want to engage with that work.

Does the idea of joining an established company in a well-defined role appeal to you? Are you looking for the flexibility of being a contract or "gig" worker? Do you have the expertise to be a consultant or interim executive? Is being a short-term or temporary worker appealing? Would you like to own and operate a franchise of a successful brand? Are you motivated to start your own business venture?

Many factors go into making this decision. You may find that the way you want to work evolves over time. My advice to job seekers and career changers is to *remain open to all these possibilities.* You may get a foot in the door of a company you admire by taking on a temporary position. Perhaps the freedom you enjoy as a gig worker loses its value when you start a family and want greater income security and benefits. The variety of challenges and work environments experienced by consultants or interim executives hired to address specific company issues might hold great appeal. You may not feel ready to start your own business but instead want to learn the ropes of business management by becoming part of a well-run franchising operation. The key question to ask, regardless of your chosen path, is will this next step ultimately lead to your Buffalo?

Starting your own business is high risk with the potential for high reward, but it is not for everybody. It's useful to bear in mind, though, that starting a successful business does not mean coming up with something that has never been done before. Starbucks did not invent selling coffee. But they did create a new way of customizing the coffee drinking experience and offering customers a "third place" to spend time that was neither home nor the workplace. Businesses succeed when they find novel ways of solving customer problems and filling customer needs. If you have a better idea, if you see a way to improve an existing product or service, you may have the basis for a profitable enterprise. I am also a strong supporter of the franchise platform. There are thousands of business opportunities with a proven model and the support to substantially reduce the risk of starting a new business.

Your dream position, your Buffalo, may not be 100 percent available to you today. But if you are willing to consider a number of paths to reach your destination, you are much more likely to get there eventually.

Targeting Your Search

You may have been feeling stale and not terribly motivated in your current position for some time. Let's assume you are looking for a new role. You may be able to change direction and find advancement by reconsidering a job function you excelled at further back in your career. With a little research and study, you could relearn and hone a previous skill that might enable you to move to another functional area in your present company or transition to a new employer.

Another avenue to take in finding job satisfaction is turning a passion you have into a career. Conduct research on the viability of your hobby by scouring the Internet. For companies in that discipline, view sample job descriptions and open opportunities and research compensation ranges. Most likely you will have to begin in a ground-floor position to demonstrate your potential, but if you can afford the time and the reduced income, this may be right for you.

Your research may have uncovered multiple industries that encompass the same sphere of work, so do not rule out other options. For instance, if you have experience as a cost accountant, you could seek opportunities in public accounting, banking, manufacturing, distribution, et cetera. Your exact role or level should also be ascertained. If you have experience as a cost accountant, do you want to remain a cost accountant, or do you have supervisory and management experience? Could you seek to manage a unit or division? Having an abundance of options would certainly provide for more opportunities.

If you are looking to stay within your current industry but in a more exciting and rewarding role, two ways to approach identifying possibilities are through exploring "concentric circles" and a related concept that I call the "career supply chain." Let me explain.

Imagine the type of target used by archers with a bow and arrow. There are bands of colorful circles, wider at the outside margin and smaller as they approach the center of the target, or "bull's-eye." Your current employer is in the bull's-eye. What other industry competitors are in that same space? These are the companies most likely to value your skills and knowledge. As you move to the next ring, what companies are similar but perhaps not at the same scale or reputation as your company? Who are your vendors and customers? Keep expanding your list as you move out on the target to include companies of lesser size, stature, or longevity. These may offer different types of opportunity. For instance, are there startups on the outer ring who might place tremendous value on your expertise and be able to offer you a more senior management position?

We use concentric circles to identify companies within your same industry. The career supply chain, on the other hand, encourages you to consider companies in *related industries* who may also value your expertise and hold your next great opportunity. For example, if you are in the automotive industry, there are numerous related companies that form part of the supply chain that encompasses all the stages from raw materials to consumers. These companies may be involved in acquiring raw materials, converting raw materials into parts, assembling parts, completing the finished products, distribution, and ultimately sales and marketing direct to consumers. Along the automotive supply chain are ancillary businesses such as equity firms and lenders, consultants, design firms, shipping companies, leasing companies, and others. Broadening your vision to include the many related companies along the supply chain increases career possibilities well worth considering.

Another key aspect to review is your customer base. What other companies are targeting your same customers? A recent client was looking to hire an experienced sales executive to sell into the large big box home stores. The client didn't really care about expertise selling a particular product. He wanted someone who knew how to open doors to the big box retailers' purchasing teams.

I encourage my clients to aim for a list of the *100 top possibilities* for their next career advancement. That may seem like a huge number, but when you combine your concentric circles with your supply chain, you'll be amazed at how many companies may be worth further investigation.

Validation of this list is important. One very effective way to further narrow your search is to commit to making what I call "advice, guidance, and counsel" calls. Similar to the way internships and volunteering can provide useful insights about specific careers, these informational phone calls tap into knowledgeable people with industry connections and insights. I suggest making these calls to mentors, coaches, and other individuals you respect within your existing network (not cold calls where possible), in order to seek their opinion. It is highly important that before you call, you are well researched. Google their name and their company—is there anything newsworthy to mention? Since you already have some level of familiarity with these people, use your best judgment to know if it would be more effective to send an email or text asking to set up a call, or if it's best to skip the email and go right to a phone call. In both instances, if your request is brief, respectful of their time, focused, and polite, most professional people are pleased to offer their opinions and advice.

Here is a basic example for an informational call:

"Good morning, (their name), my name is (your name). Your name was given to me by a friend (identify by name, if appropriate) as someone who may be able to help me build my (knowledge or network) in the _____ industry.

(Assuming you didn't schedule the call) "Is this a good time to speak? Do you have a few moments to answer some questions?"

If this is not a good time, politely inquire if they could suggest a better time for a brief conversation with you. If they answer "yes," be ready to offer a brief description of your background and situation.

You might direct the conversation like this:

"I have worked in _____ for ____ years specializing in _____. I am eager to understand where I could apply my skills and any insights you may have."

"How did you get into the _____ industry?"
"What do you like about it? What do you not like?"
"What companies would be good to look at?"
"Is your company hiring?"
"Who do you know in the industry who would be good for me to talk to?"

At this point, if you feel things are going well and you have established some rapport, make your next ask; it's an important one.
"Would you be willing to make an introduction?"

The knowledge you gain from these calls helps you to add to your potential target list or perhaps delete some of the companies you have on there. This process may also provide you with introductions or at least contact names for people with hiring authority within some of the companies on your list.

Armed with this additional information, go deeper into your research, this time using some of the many resources on the Internet. Consider using free sites like Google. Social networking sites may also provide you with links and references to employers, so consider viewing LinkedIn, Facebook, or Glassdoor. What you are especially looking for here are any factors that may provide connections between you and the people in positions to hire. Are you both alumni of the same universities or colleges? Do you have common hobbies or interests? Do you belong to any of the same trade organizations or professional associations? Are you from the same hometown? Do you root for the same teams?

Throughout your research, maintain a spreadsheet or list of companies with columns to indicate key information. Use one column to track any contact you have had with key people within the company.

Don't ignore the websites of the companies you are most interested in. Reading their recent press releases can tell you about future plans for geographic expansion or new acquisitions that could signal an opportunity for bringing on new talent. Of course, you can also view their Job Listings to learn more about existing openings, requirements, and compensation. Compensation information is currently undergoing a major shift, since several states have recently enacted pay transparency legislation requiring employers to post salary ranges for all positions.

However, I advise my clients *not* to simply send in a résumé in response to posted jobs. Submitting your application to a generic email address is almost always a waste of time, leading to frustration and discouragement when you hear nothing in return. These inboxes are flooded with résumés, and it is virtually impossible to make yours stand out from the masses. If one of your target companies posts an interesting role, follow the steps outlined previously. Find a key person or contact in the company and call them. When they mention an opening, ask for details. "That sounds interesting, can you tell me more about it?" You are actually interviewing for the role!

Your goal is to determine at least one hundred companies to contact in your job quest. From each of those companies, you will need at least three to five people to contact. This will give you a list of three hundred to five hundred people to call. We will be reviewing key performance indicators or metrics for evaluating these calls later, but it is a cold, hard fact that executive recruiters have to contact at least one hundred people a day to actually talk to fifteen to twenty. Successful recruiters and successful sales executives know that the quantity of calls, as well as the quality, is absolutely critical.

If this is all starting to feel overwhelming, keep in mind that you may also choose a one-on-one, fee-based coaching relationship with a coach or search consultant. But if you are willing to persevere and treat directing your career as a job and not a weekend hobby, you can and will succeed.

Bottom Up Success

After nearly ten years as a mid-level executive in a top-ranked corporation, Sheri felt stuck. She was willing and able to move to a new location, and she was looking for ways to find more satisfaction in her work and move up the career ladder. Sheri dedicated herself to completing the Business Plan for Life process. Her concentric circles and career supply chain exercises gave her a list of one hundred target companies to approach. After checking out the websites and scanning for news of each company, she decided to start at the bottom of the list instead of with the top ten. Her hunch, based on what she had read, was that there might be more opportunity among the smaller companies than at those larger, more established firms.

When Sheri called me, she sounded excited and happy. "You won't believe it." she said, "but after reaching out to the ten companies at the bottom of the list, I already have three viable offers." Instead of trying to navigate her way through sprawling HR departments and jump through multiple recruiting hoops at the big firms, she was able to connect directly with CEOs at the smaller startups and early-stage companies. Sheri had a concise pitch describing the value she could bring to the smaller companies. For these smaller companies, attracting someone with Sheri's expertise held tremendous value for jump-starting their growth.

Sheri stayed true to her Buffalo. From the three offers she received, she was able to choose the opportunity that met her requirements for location, income, lifestyle, professional/personal growth, and work culture. The time and considerable effort Sheri invested in her Business Plan for Life paid off.

Think, Do, Act

I can almost hear you saying, "That's great for Sheri, but that can't happen for me." Yes. It can.

Over the years I have seen so many people overcome all sorts of long odds to find work that helped them live the life they dreamed of. It is almost never easy, but as the saying goes, "That's why they call it work."

I completely believe that the methodology you are learning and practicing as you answer the Where's Your Buffalo? question will enable you to take charge of your career. You can move from being a random job seeker to a proactive hunter among many to a standout individual confident in their abilities and the value they bring to the employer lucky enough to hire them.

You must take three major steps to get there: Think/Do/Act.

So far in this chapter you have completed the very hard work to *think*—about your past, your current situation, your future hopes, dreams, and aspirations. You've been honest with yourself and have checked in with those you trust to help you gain a better understanding of who you are, what you want to become, and what it may take to achieve your goals. You've brought significant others into your process to be sure your Business Plan for Life enables them to meet their goals as well. Compromises are part of the process.

I've asked you to *do* quite a bit, starting with substantial research to reality check your ideas and targets. To solicit insider information on target roles, industries, and specific companies. To do your own "field research" by volunteering, interning, or taking a part-time position to learn more about specific careers. To go somewhere that is probably far outside your comfort zone by making contact by phone with those who may be in a position to help your search or even hire you.

There is more to *do* that I'll share in the followings chapters: building and growing your professional network and marketing yourself in a digital world. From there we move into *act*: preparing for and completing a successful interview and making a smooth transition to a new role. But before we move on from the planning stage, I want to go back to what I earlier referred to in sailing terminology as "tacking."

Rarely do we set a course—on Lake Erie or in life—that is a direct line with no setbacks or detours. Sometimes you have to take a different route or be more patient than you'd hoped with your progress. As you move through the complete Where's Your Buffalo? methodology, keep in mind that "tacking" should be expected. Keep evaluating each career move to see if it gets you closer to your Buffalo. Don't be afraid to say "no" to offers that take you in the opposite direction. Stay focused on leveraging each opportunity to advance you to that final destination. But bear in mind that your plans can and should adjust as you learn more and move through your life.

Sometimes your Buffalo might change. Sometimes getting 85 percent of what you hoped for is plenty.

The goal is to help you to be ever mindful of all the things that are really important to you as you consider a career change. To bring us back to where we started in this chapter, you begin by identifying your big rocks. As you build your plan, the big rocks are the first ones in your jar. Once they are in place (at least mostly!), the rest becomes easy. Too often we lose track of our big rocks because life goes by so fast. With your sights set on your Buffalo, and all your big rocks on board, you're sailing in a direction of what is most important in your personal and professional life.

Before you can move on, you need to be able to articulate your Buffalo. Chapter 3 will ask you to make a clear statement that will serve as your Buffalo elevator pitch.

Cultivating a Career-Focused Community

I want to open chapter 3 with a promise: if you put in the effort to complete chapter 2, I guarantee that the hardest part of the Where's Your Buffalo? program is behind you. Once you know your Buffalo, you've got a steady, warm wind in your sails.

Being thoughtful and honest about what matters to you most, what skills and abilities you have, and what you are willing to do to advance your career is very hard work. But unless you really understand yourself and your situation, it's literally impossible to take charge of your career. And no one else can help you. You'll drift and bob from job to job. Whenever anyone asks me for help, the first thing I need to know is a clear idea of exactly what they think is the next step in their career.

My main goal is to help you to *redefine yourself.* Using the WYB Business Plan for Life methodology transforms you from being a *reactive job seeker* (will someone please hire me?) to being a *proactive job hunter* (which company will be the most excited about the value I bring to their organization?).

Before you can act on your Business Plan for Life, you must be crystal clear about your Buffalo. Using everything you've learned about yourself so far, carefully complete the following statement describing your Buffalo. It can be anything you want, as long as it aligns with what you know to be true about yourself. Make sure your "big rocks" are represented and your industry is focused. You don't have to be too specific yet about earnings, but be sure to touch as clearly as possible on each of these essential elements:

1. location
2. income potential (short- and long-term)
3. lifestyle
4. professional/personal growth

Please fill in the blanks for this statement describing your Buffalo.

"I am seeking a position as a _____ in the _____ industry located in _____(city or region). I would like to work for an organization of_____(size) that enables me to work _____ (onsite, remotely, hybrid). I am interested in companies that align with my interests and/or values supporting _____."

Okay. Now we are getting somewhere. We can move on to a topic that always freaks people out: building a powerful network. I know I told you the hardest part of the WYB program is behind you, but that doesn't mean you won't have to put in more effort. You do. But if you continue to follow the insights and tips of the WYB method, your hard work *will* pay off.

Numbers Are Not a Network

Whenever I bring up "networking," people immediately tense up. They imagine that I am going to ask them to walk into a roomful of strangers, go up to people, and introduce themselves, then struggle to make small talk and a good impression. That is not my idea of networking. Even though I've spent many successful years as an executive search consultant, I dread facing those rooms full of strangers. And frankly, I don't believe the pain and effort is worth it.

When I talk about networking, I mean something very different. Genuine, effective networking is not about claiming to have fifty thousand names in your LinkedIn contacts or thousands of followers in your social media outlets. **Real networking is about developing and maintaining relationships with people in your industry who can help you reach your career goals.** It's what I'm calling a career-focused community. Because a community suggests more than a list of names; it suggests people with ongoing, engaged, *mutually beneficial relationships.*

Think for a minute about the people in your neighborhood. You probably know some better than others. Are there one or two who you have helped over the years in some way, like receiving a package for them, or keeping an eye on their house when they're on vacation? Maybe they've loaned you a tool or fed your cat? It's a two-way street of give-and-take, though neither of you is keeping score. But you know you can count on them, and they can count on you. They are part of your *personal community.*

Then there's the neighbor who only comes around when they need something from you. Can you water my plants, or give me a lift, or recommend a plumber? You want to be a good neighbor, but as the requests pile up you are less enthusiastic about helping. That doesn't make you a bad person, it just means you're human. We all suffer sometimes from the fatigue of constant giving.

It works the same way in business. When a plum job opportunity comes to me as an executive search consultant, I don't go first to the people who never return my calls or the ones who always say "no." I take the offer to the people I have reciprocal relationships with; the ones who stay in touch, offer their help when asked, and clearly value our connection. As you build your career-focused community, I encourage you to *think and act* like a recruiter.

Take a critical look at the people you consider to be your "network." Ask yourself how strong a connection you have. When was the last time you were in contact? Did you do them a favor, or did they help you in some way? Are these people you simply like, or are they people who through their position or connections may be able to advance your career aspirations?

It's great to have a group of good and reliable friends but these are not your *professional* network. To help advance your career, you also need to cultivate a wide and well-connected network of professionals.

Relationship Returns on Investment

Many years ago, a young man early in his career worked with me to help him find a next level position. That placement turned out well for him and over time he moved up within the organization. He had found his Buffalo. Although he didn't need career help, we kept in touch. Over the years we got to know about each other's families, hobbies, and our shared interests. I would occasionally turn to him for referrals, and he was able to send some candidates my way.

There was no set pattern to our contacts, but because he was part of my customer relationship management (CRM) system, I made sure to reach out at least annually, even if just to check in on his status, offer my help in any way, and see how his family was doing.

After almost twenty years since the start of our professional relationship, I was looking to fill a very attractive senior position in his industry. Naturally, he was the first person I reached out to even though I did not think he would be interested. As far as I knew, he was well settled in his community and wouldn't be willing to move. I called him because his broad network connections might help me to find the right candidate for this opportunity in another state.

As it turns out, his daughter had recently moved to the Washington, D.C., area, where this new position was based. He was contemplating a next career move but hadn't yet begun looking. My call connected him to exactly the type of position and company he hoped to find. It was an instant win-win. We both had made the effort to continually nurture our relationship as active members in our career-focused community, and it paid off.

Where to Start Looking

How do you go about identifying the people who can help you advance your career? This type of network is not about who you already know socially or casually, although you may have a core of people already in a position to help you. It's about *widening* your career community. Let's go back to two concepts from chapter 2: concentric circles and the industry supply chain.

In chapter 2, you used the concentric circles process (remember the bull's-eye image?) to identify companies within your industry that might be suitable targets for your next position. For a quick reminder, your closest competitor companies are in the smallest center circle. The next larger circle out represents companies that are related but perhaps not of the same scale or reputation. And so on as you extend the circles to the next tiers of companies you would consider working for.

The other area for exploration is the industry supply chain—that is, all the companies that supply goods and/or services to your industry. Spend some time mapping the points of contact that show how the industry you are currently in is dependent on other companies for raw materials, finished parts, financing, insurance, legal services, marketing, and technology support. It should be a long list of related companies who would appreciate the core industry knowledge you possess.

Remember that your goal was to list at least one hundred companies to contact in your job quest. After you've listed the company names, begin to list key individuals within those companies who may be in a position to either hire you or support you for a future position. From each of those one hundred companies, you will need at least three to five people to contact. This will give you a list of three hundred to five hundred people to call. You'll want to plan to call more than one person in the company to get a fuller picture of the organization, ideally from people in various parts of the business related to your skill set. *The most important part is getting started.* Begin your list with a possible first company. This is a list that you will continue to build over time.

In chapter 2, I encouraged you to reach out to these people for "insider information" about the company itself. Your task was to introduce yourself but mostly to listen to the responses each person gave about their experience with the company. If they tell you positive things about the company, you've got some validation that this is a target worth pursuing. If, on the other hand, their comments come across as negative about any important aspects of the work environment or company stability, by all means cross it off your list. Keep in mind that as a *job hunter* you are not looking for any place that will hire you. You are actively looking for the position that will be your Buffalo, the career in a company that will keep you positive, energized, and rewarded by your work.

These informational calls might also serve as a first step in building your network because now you have the beginnings of a relationship with the people who have generously taken your call and shared their advice and insights.

In addition to those who you reached in your early investigation of company targets, think about people you may have met through industry meetings, conferences, trade shows, and working groups. Pull up the company website for each of your target companies and search their directory of key management staff. Use LinkedIn to find more details on any individuals who might be helpful to you. Use this readily available information to find things you may have in common with this stranger. Human beings are social creatures who are always looking for connections. You may think you have nothing in common but even the smallest of connections can be a point of intersection.

There is no excuse for making uninformed calls anymore. Reaching out to a person without having done some basic research about them is inexcusable when so much data is public. Find a point of connection before you call. You can uncover some of the typical connections by mining readily available public sources for information in areas such as: Are you both alumni of the same university or college? Do you have common hobbies or interests? Do you belong to any of the same trade organizations or professional associations? Are you from the same hometown? Do you root for the same teams? Do you know some of the same people? Did you work for the same company? Have you both achieved some distinction such as making Eagle Scout? Even if it was many years ago, these accomplishments still provide powerful connectivity and will make it more likely that the person will be willing to help you.

Genuine connections are door openers. Without them, your chances of getting someone's precious time are slim, so making the effort is worth the investment. Believe me, I know how difficult making these phone calls is for most people, especially in this time when email and texts have all but eliminated phone conversations. We all fear rejection and, let's face it, there are people who will hang up on you. They're the same ones who jump the line at the Starbucks or cut you off in rush-hour traffic. Just as that doesn't stop you from getting your morning latte or driving home at night, the fact that there are rude people out there shouldn't discourage you from making these calls. As I've said before, successful recruiters know that the *quantity* of calls, as well as the quality, is absolutely critical.

New Buffalo, Same Process

After twenty-five happy years working his Buffalo job in the hospitality industry, Brendan began to feel a shift in his energy. The day-to-day pressures of the hotel business that once excited him were beginning to take a toll. The challenges, instead of being new and rewarding, seemed endlessly repetitive. "I feel like I'm constantly solving for the same problems," Brendan told me, "and I'll just keep doing that until the day I retire. I'm not ready to settle for sameness. New challenges in a new environment would give me the boost I need to finish out my career as enthusiastically as I began it many years ago. But what options do I have at my age? Making a lateral move to another hotel, even if it's for more money, doesn't hold any appeal. I think I'm stuck. I just don't see any way out."

Brendan was suffering from limited thinking that closed down his options. When we met over breakfast to continue our conversation, I asked him to think about his network, about who was already in his career-focused community. We started with a quick Concentric Circles exercise. The "bull's-eye" of competitor hotels was not interesting to him, but as we started to extend out the circles to companies who were not hotels but would value his hotel experience, Brendan started to get excited. "Whoa, what about conference centers, events venues, universities with large dormitory facilities, new condominium developments?" Brendan was tossing out options almost faster than I could jot them down. And the list kept growing as we moved on to his industry supply chain.

The decades he'd spent in hotel management enabled him to have deep connections to all sorts of suppliers and providers, from linen companies to architects and designers. He began to see that his hotel knowledge and expertise held value for all sorts of industries who supply hotels, and to a wide variety of companies managing residential properties or complex events venues.

Brendan knew which were the good companies and, more importantly, he had cultivated relationships with key individuals at virtually every one of them. "Tom, when I came to this meeting with you this morning, I was lost. I didn't know how to start. I only knew I had to do something. Now I have a plan and we haven't even finished our pancakes yet!"

When Brendan's original Buffalo was no longer right for him, he just needed reminding that he already knew what process to follow to map a course to his new one. It had been so long since he used it that he'd forgotten the WYB methodology. Be clear about what you want, go wide and deep to identify possibilities, and start by working your vibrant career-focused community to find your next Buffalo.

Change Your Mindset

The WYB methodology provides you with a game-changing way to extend your network into something that will yield positive results. By framing your phone outreach as calls for *advice, guidance, and counsel* instead of a hiring request, the dynamics change completely. Suddenly you are not *asking* for something, you are *offering* something. Instead of calling strangers hoping to convince them to hire you, your new mindset is that you would be a very valuable addition to the right company. You want to learn more about the company to see if it might be a good fit *for you*. You are taking a proactive hunter's approach and thinking like a recruiter.

The goal in building your network is to position yourself ahead of the pack of anonymous job seekers. The reality is that *the exact job you want may not be open today*, but somewhere down the road that job will open up. Because you have already built relationships with key decision-makers in the organization, suddenly you have a sponsor, someone willing to put your name in the mix. You become top of mind and first in line for consideration. When you realize how many decisions are made based on prior relationships, you can readily see how valuable an investment building your career-focused network is.

The bottom line for proactive job hunters is about positioning themselves. *Your Buffalo job hasn't opened yet, but when it does you want to be first in line*, not buried under a pile of résumés. There's a sure way to make yourself stand out. Recruiters know that decision-makers are motivated to hire candidates when they see the candidate's potential to:

- make the company money
- save them time by increasing productivity
- make them look good within their organization
- help the company beat their competition

The term executive talent consultants use to designate the most desirable candidates in their field is *highly placeable candidate* (HPC). Using the WYB process, you can build your identity and cultivate your mindset as a highly placeable candidate.

To qualify as an HPC, you need to have most or all of the following components:

- Elite performance history
- Verifiable achievements
- Desired skill sets
- Common skill in high demand
- Unique skill that is difficult to find
- Realistic outlook about their career path and compensation
- Verifiable references

You do not want to misrepresent yourself in an effort to meet every requirement. Going back to the self-assessment and work accomplishments surveys you completed in chapter 2, spend some time writing out a description of yourself as an HPC. If the appraisal is very difficult for you to complete, ask a mentor for his or her opinion on how best to represent yourself.

Keep in mind the criteria that managers consider most important to them—making money, improving performance, winning praise for bringing in great performers, and helping the company succeed. No one hires you to give you what *you* want in a job. It's what you can do for them and for their organization that will win you the job offer.

Your script or pitch will need to highlight at least one of the ways in which you can help the decision-maker achieve their goals for profit, productivity, and performance. Considering yourself an HPC will give you access to decision-makers with whom you can hold meaningful business conversations and highlight your worth. You want to reach out to the managers and directors of the various departments that are relevant to your job search. Do not be afraid to call the president or executive vice presidents of companies. They rarely receive these types of calls.

However, you may often be transferred to human resources (HR). This doesn't have to be a dead end. The HR representative should be aware of openings throughout a company and may reveal opportunities not yet posted. In general, though, HR staff don't make hiring decisions. They implement decisions made by department or division managers with hiring authority. That's why speaking directly with a hiring manager is preferable and more likely than not, more effective. For example, you could contact the president, EVP, district manager(s), and several regional managers all from the same company. You will learn about opportunities throughout a company, the culture, goals, and current market intelligence—all incredibly valuable information.

The HPC positioning technique is the most effective way to start a dialogue with prospective employers.

Old Contacts, Fresh Options

Carey found herself in a confusing situation. She knew she wanted to open her own restaurant, but she also knew that she lacked the high-level management experience investors would be looking for. She was impatient to launch her own business, so she didn't want to enter into a multiple year contract as a senior executive for another employer. To get help finding the right opportunity, she started reviewing the many owners and executives she knew from her years in the industry, including past employers.

Carey reached out to her top few to set up informal coffee meetings, letting each person know she wanted their advice on her next career move. No pressure, just some acquaintances catching up and chatting over coffee about what was happening in their industry.

Her first meeting was with Melinda, a chef/owner she had known for years and had worked for briefly. Melinda was pivoting away from the restaurant business to start a line of gourmet frozen foods and was moving her business to South Carolina. *Interesting*, Carey thought, *and I'd learn about a different part of the food industry but joining Melinda would take me further away from my dream.*

The next meeting was with another former employer, Jacqui, who had added a retail store to her already thriving restaurant operation. Years before, Carey had worked for this dynamic entrepreneur before Jacqui opened her own restaurant. The two had stayed in touch casually, meeting up at fundraisers and other industry events over the years. Carey shared her plans to open a restaurant of her own in a small town upstate. Jacqui listened carefully, asked a bunch of questions about the plan, especially about the timing and the financing. After Carey explained that she was looking for an interim senior management position to fill in some gaps in experience, Jacqui surprised her.

"I've got a contract to write a book about my business success and the fact is I am way behind on my deadline. I just can't seem to find the time to work on the book when my businesses are so demanding. How would you feel about taking on the role of interim CEO for a year so I can finish my book?"

Out of the blue, the perfect offer and an ideal solution for Jacqui and Carey appeared. One year later, able to add CEO experience with a nationally known restaurant to her pitch deck, Carey was able to attract all the investors she needed to launch her business plan. And Jacqui's book was delivered to the publisher on time.

Developing Your Script

Whatever goal you set for your calls will determine the approach or the "script" you should follow. For those early advice, counsel, and guidance calls, you'll want to keep your description of yourself brief and tightly focused. Remember that your main goal in these calls is to initiate a relationship by doing more listening than talking.

Your remarks might go something like this example:

"*Good morning, my name is ____. I am reaching out to you because your name was given to me by a colleague (state name, if appropriate) /*

or *in my research you surfaced as a highly knowledgeable person in our industry. I am an experienced ____ with ____ years specializing in_____. I am considering shifting my focus into (or expanding my career options into) _____. I want to get your thoughts on it. From your experience, does a move like this make good business sense? Are there companies in this arena you would suggest I contact? Are there companies you'd suggest I avoid? I have been researching the ____ industry and it seems to me that it is growing at an increasing rate. Are you finding this to be accurate? Is there anyone else you can recommend I speak to? What types of positions do you have open?"*

For the next level of engagement, the HPC calls, you'll need to be prepared to do more of the talking in a concise and interesting way.

The best approach to creating a compelling presentation about yourself is to write a script and practice it multiple times. Don't try to "wing it." You should write or type your script for several compelling reasons. You will demonstrate a confident attitude. You will demonstrate that you are well prepared and have done your research. You will be better able to maintain control of the conversation. And you are far more likely to make a positive impression by staying on track.

To help you craft your most effective script, try using some of the powerful words shown here. As always, don't exaggerate but don't undersell yourself either. Make sure you choose words that fit your personality and style authentically.

Below are positive power words that can help you and your pitch stand out. And you'll also see a list of words to *avoid*. These are negative and will undermine your message of confidence, positivity, and a can-do attitude. Be as careful to avoid these as you are careful to use the power words.

Words that "sell"

- Abundant
- Achiever
- Adaptable
- Adroit
- Advance
- Advantage
- Aggressive
- Alert
- Ambitious
- Analytical
- Approve
- Articulate
- Assertive
- Astute
- Benefit
- Challenging
- Chief
- Comfort
- Conceptual
- Conscientious
- Conservative
- Cool-headed
- Cutting Edge
- Dependable
- Deserve
- Diplomatic
- Discovery
- Discuss
- Ego Drive
- Empower
- Energetic
- Enjoyable
- Enrapture
- Enthusiastic
- Ethical
- Exceptional
- Excellent
- Facilitator
- Faithful
- Fresh
- Fun
- Goal-oriented
- Guarantee
- Happiness
- High Degree
- High Level/Standard
- Highly Regarded
- Independent
- Innovative
- Insight
- Inspiring
- Integrity
- Intelligence
- Keen
- Manner
- Money
- Negotiation Skills
- On-track
- Opportunity
- Optimum
- Overwhelming
- Persuasive
- Planning Ability
- Polish
- Political Savvy

- Positive Pragmatism
- Proactive
- Promotable
- Proud
- Proven
- Recommendable
- Refreshing
- Reliable
- Resilient
- Resourceful
- Responsible
- Results
- Results-oriented
- Security
- Self-Awareness
- Self-Directed
- Self-Reliant
- Self-Starter
- Sensible
- Sociable

- Solution
- Speech
- Stable
- Strategic
- Strategic Thinker
- Strong
- Style
- Substantial
- Successful
- Superlative
- Surmount
- Team Builder
- Team Leader
- Team Player
- Tenacity
- Tough-minded
- Trusted
- Understanding
- Value
- Vision
- Vital

Words to Positively Describe Personality

- Analytical
- Arresting
- Candid
- Compelling
- Comprehensive
- Creative
- Detailed
- Durable
- Exhaustive
- Explosive

- Faithful
- Fascinating
- Great
- Hardworking
- Heady
- Heavyweight
- In-depth
- Incisive
- Innovative
- Intriguing

- Limitless
- Lively
- Methodical
- No-nonsense
- Panoramic
- Practical
- Professional
- Rugged
- Sound

- Stable Sweeping
- Striking
- Strong
- Tough
- Trusted
- Unswerving
- Vibrant
- Vivid

Words to Describe Real Results

- Builds Motivation
- Corrects
- Creates
- Cuts Through
- Dramatic
- Effective
- Fixes
- Lowers
- Overwhelming

- Pays off
- Provides
- Protects
- Raises
- Reduces
- Restores
- Revitalized
- Stops

Words to *Avoid*

- Bad
- But
- Buy
- Cannot
- Cost
- Deal
- Death
- Difficult
- Fail
- Failure
- Hard

- Hurt
- Liability
- Liable
- Lose/Loss
- Manipulate
- Maybe
- Might
- Might be
- Obligation
- Perhaps
- Probability

- Price
- Sharp
- Should
- Sign
- Sold

- Super
- Try
- Will not
- Worry
- Ya know

None of this is easy to do. You want to avoid having your delivery sound robotic or insincere, yet you have to be concise and clear. Work at delivering your remarks in a natural, conversational manner. By not rushing or speaking in a monotone, your delivery will be much more effective. You may even want to make a practice video of yourself, including watching your facial expressions. Try it out with a friend, family member, or trusted colleague who will give you honest feedback. This is a rehearsal, just as if you were going to be performing onstage or delivering a speech. Apple founder Steve Jobs was famous for his apparently off the cuff, relaxed presentations to the Apple staff. In fact, he spent weeks relentlessly improving his script and his "casual" delivery by practicing over and over again until he could communicate his message in a powerful yet natural, conversational way.

Try composing your presentation with some dramatic flair, because you'll need to grab the decision-maker's attention. The first few minutes—sometimes seconds—of any dialogue sets the tone and direction and is central to the success of the entire conversation.

Your script has to have some sizzle or be a "grabber." Just like in school when you learned to structure a paragraph with an introduction, a body, and a "close" or conclusion, your HPC script should contain the same elements. Your introduction explains who you are, who referred you (if applicable), and the reason for your call. The body of your script contains what I refer to as your SAVE information—it describes your skills, accomplishments, and value, and provides examples. And the close is whatever call to action or next step you have planned as a result of this conversation.

Elements of Your SAVE

Let's take a closer look at the main content of your script, the SAVE. Skills are your factual, true characteristics and attributes. For example, years of experience, education, work history, title(s), certifications, type of job, and basic duties are all considered **skills**.

The **accomplishments** are things that you are proud of, where you used your skills described above to make something useful happen. Remember, you listed those achievements as part of your work history in chapter 2, so go back and review your list.

The **value** is what the future employer would receive if they hired you. It could be evident by the value you provided to your past employer, or a solution you created to solve a tough problem. To get the hiring manager to truly listen to you, you'll need to clearly answer the question of, "What's in it for them?"

Try using a linking statement that starts with one of these phrases to state your value proposition.

- What this means for you is
- This is important to you because
- You can expect
- As you can imagine
- This will add
- This will improve
- This will solve
- This will meet your needs by
- This will help you accomplish
- The advantage is
- This would enable me to
- The benefit to you is
- The impact would be
- The bottom line is

Taken together, the SAVE statements concisely express the value that you can bring to your next employer. You can drive home the point by using specific *measurable and quantifiable* **examples** from your past work experience.

Here are a few examples of SAVE statements:

"Hi, [first name]. This is [full name]. I wanted to introduce myself to you as a top marketing executive who structured and delivered marketing strategies that significantly lowered customer acquisition costs and increased sales per customer by 28 percent. I can have an immediate impact on your organization's ability to win in the market. How do you see a unique talent such as mine helping you with your company's marketing initiatives?"

"Hi, [first name]. This is [full name], and I am a dynamic and aggressive IT professional. I recently saved my former employer an estimated $1.3 million dollars annually by integrating new telephone systems, computer networks, and customer tracking applications. Through reducing costs and increasing profits through innovative technology, I could have the same impact on your organization. Would you be interested in meeting with me?"

"Hi, [first name]. This is [full name]. I saw in the business news that your company is expanding into my hometown. I have five years' experience and within just the past six months, I saved my current employer $325K in labor costs alone. I was able to accomplish this by simplifying the way we brought supplies to the plant floor. The advantage to you in hiring me would be my immediate capability of producing outstanding results with little or no training time and expense."

Keep in mind as you write your script: skills tell, value sells. Be careful not to just recite a list of skills without clearly stating the measurable and real value your skills delivered!

Not Ready for HPC?

If you feel overwhelmed by the HPC model and want to get some practice with a softer style, the Opening Dialogue Approach (also called the 4 I's, from the Acclivus R3 Sales®[1] program) might be a better fit for you. This conversational model is intended to increase the probability and potential for establishing trust and legitimacy with a new contact. The goal here is to leave a lasting and positive impression.

The four actions key to making yourself memorable in a good way are:

- Introduce
- Insight
- Inspire
- Invest

In the **introduce** segment, you greet the prospective employer by name and then briefly identify yourself. Keep it short and sweet, answering the questions, "Who are you?" and "Why are you calling?" You begin by saying, "I am _____" or "I do _____."

Example:

"Hello, Mrs. Smith. My name is Alex Ramos with XYZ. I am responsible for developing business relationships with key clients in the construction industry."

For the second action, **insight,** you want to demonstrate your insider knowledge about the company. Preparation is the basis for insight. Your statements should enable you to answer the employer's likely questions, "What do you know about me, the company, my position, or my industry?" Begin with an "I" statement: "I understand,"; "I've read," or "I've noticed that you . . ."

---

1   Acclivus R3 Solutions. https://acclivus.com/services/#r3-curriculum. Accessed February 1, 2024.

Example:

"Mrs. Smith, I noticed in the trade journal *Commercial World* that your company won a large contract to build five luxury hotels in the next two years."

To **Inspire,** try to elicit a positive response from the person you've contacted. You'll want to overcome their reluctance to give you their time by answering their implied questions: "Why should I listen to you?" and "Why is this of value to me?" To address these critical but often unspoken questions, you need to have done your research about the prospect, his/her position, new developments in their business, and/ or general industry trends.

Example:

"As a former construction project manager, I focused on large scale projects in various locations. Hiring an experienced lineman like me who is adept in both state and local regulations will be a critical component in the development of your team."

For the final segment, **invest,** propose an action which will indicate investment or commitment on the part of the prospect. Answer the questions, "What do you expect from me?" and "How will we spend our time together?" Make it specific: who, what, when, where, and how. Also make it mutual, requiring participation by the prospect as well as by you.

Example:

"I am confident that a thirty-minute conversation would allow both of us to gain further insight into some of your current challenges and some of the ways I've helped companies with a large-scale project overcome similar challenges. Would this be a good use of our time?"

Here's another example of a concise opening dialogue approach:

"Hello, [first name]. This is [name]. I am an experienced packaging sales professional. I recently read in *USA Today* that your company is introducing a reinforced tape with a tamper-evident seal, which will be especially important to shippers of luxury goods, foods, and pharmaceuticals. My experience in selling such products helped increase my former employer's sales by 67 percent. I'm calling to see how I might help you develop your sales staff for the launch of this product. Is this a good time to discuss your challenges?"

Whichever approach you use for introducing yourself to a prospective employer or sponsor, it has to comfortably fit your style and personality. Trying to act like someone you are not will be unsustainable. You may need to create several versions of your presentation and make dozens of calls to see how people respond to your words and how to achieve the right flow. Change, adapt, and refine after each call to see what gets you the best results.

Don't Forget to Close

The final component of any script is the **close**. After grabbing the decision-maker's attention and wowing them with your SAVE or using the opening dialogue approach, you must ask an effective closing question. Too often people miss this step and, as a consequence, miss an opportunity to continue the relationship. Based on how the conversation has evolved, you may choose to ask something along the lines of the following:

- What would be the first step in getting us together?
- Where could you see an individual of my caliber in your organization?
- Have I told you enough to interest you in setting up a meeting now, or would you like to hear more?

Target Times and Call Counts

A successful job hunter knows how to plan her time accordingly. Planning is about carefully organizing the current day's work and preparing for the following day. Preparation is the key to the kingdom in job searches. Yet, in the course of a busy day with pressing, urgent matters to address, planning is typically the first necessity to be abandoned. Unfortunately, a very common and altogether apt expression is: "failing to plan is planning to fail."

Daily planning requires time, thought, and discipline. Unfocused planning results in a lack of production. Efficient plans are structured, written out, and committed to in your schedule or daily planner. Success comes to those who organize, plan, and prioritize their calls each day. This means taking time each day to type or write the list of who you are planning to call tomorrow and preparing your scripts ahead of time.

Executive recruiters have earmarks known as "prime time" or "golden hours." These are the times when you are more likely to reach decision-makers. Decision-makers are typically in their offices early in the morning and late in the afternoons. They even work weekends! If you want a job, you need to be working the same hours as the decision-makers. The "golden hours" are not the time to be spending on the Internet conducting personal research. It probably goes without saying that if you are currently employed, you should not be participating in such activities at your current place of employment.

If you're not currently employed or are a "free agent," you should be devoting yourself to your job hunt as if it were your full-time job. The more time you invest, the faster your efforts will result in a new position.

In a perfect world, you are making fifty to one hundred outbound connection attempts a day. Start small and build each day. A person actively networking without a job should be trying to connect with at least one person a day. The more conversations you have in a day, the better. Consistent and steady activity is the key.

This does not include speaking with an administrative assistant. This does not include attending a networking meeting with forty-five people. Networking meetings are helpful to make connections and learn new names, but you need to be on the phone pitching yourself to decision-makers. Hitting a minimum of fifteen connections a day will be tough. If you are not meeting this expectation, someone else looking for a job is. Remember, you have lots of competition!

In the current economy especially if you are a "free agent" who is currently unemployed, developing your connections should be taken as seriously as if it were a job. The time you spend is an investment. This is hard work. It is an activity-driven process and it all comes down to numbers. The more activity you engage in by connecting with people for a coffee, through an email, or making a new connection on LinkedIn, the more likely you are to find the opportunity you desire. Through WYB, you can access activity sheets for you to use on a daily, weekly, and monthly basis to track your progress. Using these will help you keep going by giving you a sense of achievement.

You can never do too many targeted outreach efforts, and by that I do *not* mean sending out two hundred blind résumés to online job postings. Depending on how much time you have available, you should aim to make some meaningful connections each week. Set a realistic goal for yourself, like securing two to three interviews or meetings a week. If you continue this pace for several months, you should be able to land a job. However, if you are tracking only a few calls or emails a week, it will take you much longer. These results are proven. More targeted activity leads to quicker results. This is how we as executive talent consultants know our business is statistically sound.

Also, realistically, most of your calls and contacts will not be positive. You will encounter rejection and resistance. Your ability to overcome those discouraging moments will be crucial. Being prepared, maintaining a positive outlook, and adjusting as you go to improve your performance will help you stay on track.

Things to Always Do

This chapter contains a lot to think about as you prepare to start expanding your focused network and building meaningful relationships.

WYB is all about business, but business is conducted by human beings. No matter what role you are seeking, no matter how much or how little experience you have, there are some general guidelines to practice. Here are some helpful hints to keep in mind as you reach out to others in your field.

- Listening skills are more important than speaking/writing skills.
- In any powerful conversation, you should talk only about 30 percent of the time. By asking good questions you should enable the decision-maker to respond while you listen attentively for the remaining 70 percent of the conversation.
- Develop a vocabulary that creates a vivid picture for the listener or reader (see word lists).
- Avoid jargon or slang, whether company jargon or general jargon. The other person may not understand you or think you are trying to appear hip.
- Be positive. Never say "possibly," "maybe," "I think that could be." Instead use "yes," "certainly," "always," and "of course."
- Have the courage of your convictions.
- Use a warm tone of voice.
- Smile. Even though a smile can't be seen over the phone (though of course it can be seen on Zoom!), smiling changes the tone and energy of the conversation.
- Remember, enthusiasm is contagious.

We Have All Been in This Meeting

At our weekly staff meeting, the managing director asks each team leader for their updates. What's going well, what's in jeopardy, what's in the pipeline. As each person delivers their report, it's easy to tell from the relaxed atmosphere in the room that things are going really, really well for our division. Lots of smiles, accolades, and attaboys to go around. We're a strong team of high performers who support each other in all the work laid out in our annual plan. The group is anticipating closing out the fiscal year with a strong performance and most likely a bonus.

As we prepare to return to our offices, the managing director tells us she has an announcement to make. Casting a meaningful look at our IT director, Mateo, she breaks the news that Mateo has given notice and will be taking a top job with one of our competitors.

Mateo has been part of our team since the beginning and has the trust and confidence of all of us. Losing him is a big blow and comes at a bad time since we are about to do significant systems upgrades before year-end. The managing director gets right to the point. "We need to move fast to fill this position with the right person." She asks each of us point-blank, "Who do you know who might be a great fit for our team?"

Before the job gets posted internally, before it appears on the company website, and long before it goes out on various online job sites, the search is on. That's when your outreach and your career focused network building pay off. One of the team members speaks up. "I've had a couple of conversations with someone who might be just the person we need. Let me reach out to them and see if we can set up a meeting."

Build a Community for Life

If you frame each of these calls as a friendly, professional, and respectful conversation, many strangers may be willing to listen and engage. From a list of three hundred to five hundred potential people, you may reach one hundred, or maybe only forty to fifty. Through this process you are now known by and at least lightly connected to individuals who can become part of your relevant career community.

But don't reach out to somebody just once and consider them a valuable contact or a viable relationship. It's up to you to create your own CRM (customer relationship management system) even if it is a simple spreadsheet to make sure you nurture and refresh these relationships over time.

Be sure to send a thank-you email or better yet a handwritten note after your initial phone call. Follow up where appropriate by passing along articles or links that might be of interest to them. Respond to things your new connections post through LinkedIn. Check in periodically to share your updates or ask for theirs. Offer your assistance. Make sure there is always *value for them* in every communication.

One of the biggest mistakes people make is to stop building their network once they've got a great position. You need to work on building your network continuously throughout your career. Be extra engaged when you've got a great position that enables you to help others.

Creating and nurturing your career-focused community is a lifelong process that ideally begins when you are a student and continues until retirement (and maybe even after that!). Yes, it is work, but it will definitely be rewarding. And it can even be great fun getting to know and like more people across your industry.

My final thought—and this is very important—I always ask everyone I talk to "how can I help you?" This makes the conversation easy and comfortable because I will genuinely always try to help everyone in any way I can.

CHAPTER 4

Marketing Yourself in a Digital World

This chapter could consist of the shortest, most succinct piece of advice anyone has ever given you: when it comes to creating your digital identity, let common sense guide you. Merriam-Webster defines common sense as "sound and prudent judgment based on a simple perception of the situation or facts" and goes on to cite a relevant example, quoting James Poniewozik, journalist and TV critic for the *New York Times*, who recently claimed, "So far, I've had the common sense not to tweet anything ghastly."[2] Notice that even this world-class journalist cautions that "so far" he has avoided or perhaps outlasted the temptation to tweet something he would later regret.

The many avenues open to us on social media represent anything but a simple situation, especially when these communications are instantaneous, mostly unretractable, and can do enough damage to a reputation or brand to deserve the term *viral*. As the revered investor and philanthropist Warren Buffett observed, "It takes 20 years to build a reputation and five minutes to ruin it. If you think about that, you'll do things differently."

---

2   "Common sense." Merriam-Webster.com Dictionary, Merriam-Webster, https://www.merriam-webster.com/dictionary/common%20sense. Accessed 1 February 2024.

I realize it's not enough for me to advise the people I work with, especially those college graduates recently entering the job market, to just use their common sense. Instead, let's start by reflecting on the process of applying for work and how the Internet has changed the rules. I'll share some short illustrations of the fallout that can occur from unthinking, casual use of social media.

People, Not Algorithms, Make Hiring Decisions

For anyone who didn't grow up on a farm they were going to inherit or who wasn't raised knowing they would eventually take over their family business, looking for work has always been hard. Nepotism— that is, the informal system of relatives and friends helping their relatives and friends—used to smooth the way for some: if your uncle worked for the railroad, chances were he could "get you in" with an entry-level railroad job. There's no denying that it's still difficult today to find the *right position in the right company,* but let me reminisce for a bit that it used to be much harder.

The Bad Old Days

We have to go back to the dark ages before the Internet. When I was in college looking for work, the search started with the newspaper. Yes, the local printed paper had pages of Want Ads. These were usually brief descriptions of available positions, often with no information about salary. They included a mailing address and sometimes a phone number to call. I'd circle the interesting ones in red pen.

Like all other job seekers, I'd been told how absolutely critical it was to have a polished, professional résumé. Everyone looking for work spent hours toiling over these documents that we painstakingly typed up on a typewriter. If you made a mistake, you had to paint over it with correction fluid or rip out the page and start over. Next you took this page to a printer who had to typeset the document. It seems no matter how careful you were, when you paid for your one hundred copies and opened the box, you discovered you'd managed to misspell your own name. Off you went, back to the printer to shell out more precious dollars.

You had one version of a résumé intended to somehow appeal equally to the wide variety of employers you'd be reaching out to. The result was inevitably either too generic to be meaningful or too specific to be very useful for wide distribution. In my case, with very little to share other than working as a bartender or a valet parking attendant to pay for my education, I turned spring break into a "Religious retreat for 25 young men."

No matter. After circling the most appealing jobs in the newspaper want ads, you'd put your résumé in an envelope. If you were really dedicated, you might enclose a somewhat more customized cover letter, then you'd mail it off to the company. Usually the result, as you would expect, was silence. It was common for job seekers then to say, "I may as well be dropping my résumé into the trash can instead of the mailbox." It was a very broken, frustrating system.

Computer technology and the age of the Internet created so many better ways to access and share information. But there are pitfalls too.

Shortly after the Monster.com website made a splash on the Internet as a public job board, one of Monster's founders addressed the national annual meeting of executive recruiters. I was in the audience waiting to hear about this new employment marketplace. "Gentlemen," he began, "it's a whole new game for employers and employees. You all better start thinking about what you'll do next because in less than two years, your jobs, the entire field of recruiting, will no longer exist."

Like many predictions, that didn't happen. Why not? Because even with the power of the Internet, hiring is still a very human process that, when done successfully, requires significant human interaction.

Think about it. Why do employers hire people? To solve a problem. That problem might be a need to increase production levels or design security measures or streamline financial processes. *Every person who is hiring is trying to find the person who can best solve their specific problem and provide the best value to the company.* The whole idea of hiring centers around *risk*. The candidates who are less risky—those who are the most likely to contribute to the success of the company—are the ones who land and keep the best jobs. The employer responsible for hiring is looking for the absolute best candidate; ninety-nine out of one hundred are not going to get the job. The manager is not looking for a reason to hire everyone, he or she's looking for reasons *not* to hire *you*!

This is where the thoughtful, carefully curated management of your image across all media becomes so important. I say "all media" because *everything* you do contributes to the image an employer forms about you. It's not just selfies on Facebook.

Accentuate the Positive

A good place to start is with a personal inventory of your digital presence. List all the ways you participate in digital communication. Email. Voicemail. Texts. LinkedIn. Facebook, Instagram, Pinterest, Twitter, TikTok, et cetera. You know where you spend time on the Internet. Now think about the audiences you are trying to reach through each of these platforms. Chances are it's a mixed bag of family, friends, coworkers, potential romantic partners, and even strangers anywhere in the world who might share some of your interests.

We don't relate to family or friends the same way we interact with strangers, but the Internet erases much of the privacy protection these more personal communications used to have. In other words, if someone wants to find out what sort of employee you might be, they will scroll through as much of what you post as they can easily find.

Party Hearty

In its very early days when Facebook still only existed on a few college campuses, Sharon was accepting applications for a key position in a fine dining restaurant. On top of the pile was a résumé from a young woman who had recently graduated with a degree from an excellent hospitality program. She had extensive experience working in a variety of superior restaurants, had traveled in Europe, enjoyed cooking as a hobby, and came from a family who owned and operated a boutique hotel. She seemed to have it all.

Sharon was ready to bring her in for an interview when she happened to show the résumé to her assistant, Ben, an intern from a local university. "Have you taken a look at her Facebook posts?" Ben innocently asked. Sharon said, "Facebook? What's that?" Ben started typing on his computer keyboard. "Check it out," he said, swiveling his screen for Sharon to see. There was the candidate, dancing on a tabletop, waving a handle of vodka. More pictures of her partying filled the screen. It seemed partying was all she ever did. Sharon never made that call to set up an interview. There were plenty of other candidates eager for the job.

We like to think we've gotten more sophisticated about our use of social media, but on the other hand, maybe it's easier than ever to take it for granted since "everybody's doing it."

A word of caution about letting down your guard: recently I was sitting with a client as he reviewed the credentials for two highly qualified candidates. Both women were exceptionally strong candidates on paper. Excellent academic records, outstanding extracurricular activities that showed genuine leadership skills, and both had completed impressive initial interviews over Zoom. "It's a tough call to make," my client confided. "But then I decided to see what I could find on Facebook." One candidate seemed to have been a bridesmaid in several weddings. The photos she posted captured images of classy, happy celebrations. In every smiling photo she looked mature, composed, and joyful. The other candidate's images were of much more casual events at clubs and beaches. These photos showed her in wild costumes flaunting joke-sized glasses of wine. "When I looked at these posts, it told me how these women see themselves, or maybe how they want the world to see them," the client said. "I know what image we want our employees to project. It was an easy choice to hire the bridesmaid."

Image matters to employers, and that concern extends beyond photos to statements of belief, whether they are religious, political, or even about something "safe" like sports teams. Many corporate employers devote staff time to searching Twitter as part of the candidate screening process. Posts or statements or even emojis endorsing the statements of others can be enough to raise a red flag for risk-averse employers. You are entitled to have opinions. But as a candidate for employment, you have to put your best foot forward. Freely sharing your privately held ideas too often results in people forming preconceived and probably mistaken ideas about you.

Your digital marketing campaign has to create the kind of image you want a future employer to see. Be very careful what you put out there. Posting political or controversial material can have a profoundly negative impact on who will hire you. If it's a great job opportunity, it is going to be a very competitive process. Don't make it easy to dismiss your application.

Remember the elimination process starts early and is usually not transparent. One hiring manager I worked with shared his prescreening process with me. If there was a misspelling on the documents the candidate submitted, they were out. If they went to a college that had rejected his son, they were out. The only speeding ticket he ever got in his life happened in a nearby state. Any candidate from that state was out. Is this outrageous? Yes. Is it unfair? Definitely. But believing that things like this don't happen is naive. You have to control your message and make sure the image you project is your *best* self.

Who Are You?

Each of us has a complex network of connections. We have family, friends, coworkers, former classmates, teammates, and lots of casual acquaintances. We relate to these people in different way, and in some cases may even be known by different nicknames. But how do you want the business world to see you?

A young man came to me for career advice. In our initial conversation I started to form an impression of him as earnest, smart, and highly motivated. We scheduled a follow-up meeting for the next week. The next day I received an email from him thanking me for our session. Then I noticed his email address, and let's just say it was pretty inappropriate. Uh-oh. Next, I searched for his LinkedIn account. His profile showed him wearing a hoodie and sunglasses, looking cool but definitely not professional. When I called to confirm our meeting his voicemail opened with "Yo, Dude." These three pieces of evidence indicated we had to start his job search by helping him to craft a mature, work-ready image.

Of course, there's more to life than work. It's fine and healthy to have different ways to relate to different people in our lives. But we have to be realistic about the importance of managing our digital presence. You might consider maintaining a separate email account for your casual or personal correspondence. Have a separate phone number for professional purposes perhaps but if you only have one mobile number, be sure to update and professionalize your voice message.

In all forms of public communication, lose the things that were cool in school. Get a professional headshot. Look the part you want to be hired to fill. People who don't know you are going to judge you initially based on what they find on the Internet. And remember: things you put out on the Internet can be part of your online image forever.

Image Matters

There are many resources and tools available to build your online presence. LinkedIn is a first stop for many professionals, so let's start there. Whenever I am considering someone for executive placement, I go to their LinkedIn site and take a look. How complete is the information? For example, it sends up a red flag when someone does not put any dates on their bio. It makes me wonder what they are trying to hide. If they are hoping to mask their age as either too young (recent graduate), or too old (over fifty-five) it's a short-lived distraction. At some point, the interviewer is going to see you on Zoom or in person, so it's better to be up front about your age and target opportunities that value and seek out your experience.

Be as specific as possible about your experience, skills, education, and interests. Get someone you trust and who knows you well to read it before you post it. Ask them for advice about descriptions and wording. Does it sound like you? Are there other details you should include? Be careful, though, about doing anything so public or widely available online that signals you are "open to opportunities." If you are currently employed, you generally don't want to announce to the world (and reveal to your employer) that you are job hunting.

Above all, in every category, be completely honest.

We have seen some very public scandals in the news lately. People who should have known better have falsified their credentials. Sooner or later the truth will come out. I know of one company where a disgruntled employee felt he was unfairly passed over for a promotion. He decided to look into the background of the new hire and, in the process, unearthed falsified information that person had claimed about their qualifications. The new employee was fired for cause and now has that unfortunate incident to contend with for future employment opportunities.

Google yourself to see what comes up. Go through your list of online accounts and activities and delete, modify, or enhance to make sure they form an honest, consistent, appealing, and professional image—one that will reassure employers that hiring you is a smart move. The competition for that great position starts as soon as someone begins to view you as a candidate.

Turn the Tables

Hiring managers are going to use the Internet to make some preliminary decisions about you. You can and should be proactive about using the Internet as a discovery tool too. I've mentioned that job boards are not a valuable vehicle for finding great employment. However, they can be a good starting point for your search because they give you a glimpse of who is hiring and what positions they need to fill. Job boards are good for gathering information but sending your résumé in to them is like filing it in a black hole.

Following up the job board leads on the Internet can provide a portal for detailed information about any company you are considering applying to. Visit the company website and review the listed leadership team. Go to their LinkedIn pages. Does what you see make the company more or less attractive to you? Do you notice any possible connecting elements with the key people? Alumni affiliation? Membership in a professional organization? Volunteer activities with a charity you also support?

Google the key leaders and the company to see if anything newsworthy has happened lately. Check out Twitter or Facebook and follow someone if their posts seem interesting. And remember to keep your LinkedIn profile fresh and up to date. Posting links to articles that caught your eye can let people know you are keeping current. Adding any new certifications, activities, or work-related experiences is another way to get noticed. During your job search, you should be routinely updating LinkedIn, but don't let this practice lapse just because you're happy in a new job. It never hurts to remind your network that you're out there doing things that deserve sharing.

Old School Still Rules

There's no denying the Internet has given us many advantages. But when it comes to forming genuine connections with fellow human beings, live and in person is still the best way. Unfortunately, as we grow more accustomed to digital forms of expression, as emails are replaced by even briefer texts and DMs, for many it is becoming more awkward and uncomfortable to speak with someone directly. I recently heard a young person describe someone calling them on the phone as "rude." In the business world, though, person to person, even when working remotely, is still the most effective, productive, and valuable form of communication.

Like everything else that is hard to do, there are few people willing to make the effort. This gives you an opportunity to shine. If you practice and become skilled at verbal expression, at making direct contact with individuals clearly and succinctly, you will possess an enduring advantage that will set you apart as a candidate and an employee.

I've already spent a fair number of paragraphs extolling the virtues of well-scripted phone calls. These always begin by asking for permission to continue. "Do you have five minutes for a brief conversation?" is enough to get you started. But how do you get to that first call using online resources?

Let's go back to the company search you conducted after seeing a posting on a job board. Rather than responding to an "info" company email, try to figure out who is likely to be the person actually making the hiring decision. Check them out on LinkedIn to see if you have any connections. If you have a mutual acquaintance, ask them to make an e-introduction for you. It only takes a minute to do this sort of favor, and generally people are very willing to make connections on your behalf. If you don't have any people in common, is there anything else you share, no matter how big or small? People who have achieved a significant accomplishment like attaining an Eagle Scout rank, being named a Rhodes Scholar, or completing the Boston Marathon are often open to knowing others with the same experience. All sorts of distinguishing achievements can form lifelong bonds across generations. Whatever possible connection you come up with, lead with that in a short email with a subject line that stimulates interest. Avoid being cute or funny but try to be creative enough that even the person with the overflowing inbox will want to open your message.

But don't let this email be the start of many more emails. In this first message, ask for a phone appointment. That's a much lower risk than a face-to-face meeting and is much easier to agree to, especially when you promise to keep it short. Asking for ten minutes of someone's time is hard to refuse. Suggest some specific days and times for a call or a Zoom if they prefer—don't leave it up to the person to set it up for you. But be sure to end your suggested times with words to the effect that "if none of these times are convenient for you, please suggest a better time."

Once you've got a call scheduled, get to work on perfecting your script and delivery. You are now engaged in the process of creating a "ladder of access" where each step builds to the next. Although you are the one looking for a position, you are in a seat of power that you want to retain. This is part of the image you are establishing—an image of being in control while demonstrating your high level of responsibility, responsiveness, courtesy, and professionalism.

If at the scheduled call time you are sent to voicemail, consider it a test. Leave a polite message and make it *your* responsibility to call back. Give them a specific day and time ("I'll try you again Tuesday at 10 a.m."). You can include the option for them to return your call. "If you want to reach out to me instead, you can contact me at (provide your phone number and your email)." When you don't hear from them, but you do as you said you would by calling them on the next Tuesday, you're not "stalking" them, you're showing that you keep your word. In my line of work, I sometimes have to do these types of follow-up/ rescheduled calls two or three times before I finally get the person on the line. Generally, they are apologetic for having been so hard to reach, and as a result are often more inclined to reward my perseverance by giving me their full attention.

Following up means you stay in control of the relationship. If your call goes well, the next rung on the "ladder of access" is suggesting a meeting by Zoom or in person in order to learn more about the company's potential needs and opportunities—and simply as a low-stress, easy way to deepen and maintain a professional connection. Believe me when I tell you how very, very few job seekers do that. Part of your power is in being proactive as a job hunter, by being as professional in your approach as an executive recruiter. With every point of contact from introduction to each stage of follow-up, continue to think and act like a professional recruiter. Don't wing it. In a highly competitive market, second chances are not usually available.

The WYB program aims to help you navigate your way around the standard approach job seekers take, frustrating steps that are all part of a useless application process. It takes time, patience, and practice. But the reward of a gratifying career is out there for the ones who honestly and consistently put in their best effort.

CHAPTER 5

Crushing the Interview

Let's do a role reversal. Today you're the person behind the hiring desk. I want you to think like the hiring authority, who I sometimes call "the client." Keep in mind, I am trying to teach you to approach this process like a search consultant or recruiter. You're the candidate, but you are also the recruiter, selling yourself into the role. In this simulation, you've scheduled final interviews with the three top candidates for a key position in your company. On paper, all three applicants look very similar in quality and level of education, comparable work experience, and solid references. Which one will you decide to hire?

Candidate X

Ten minutes after our interview was scheduled to start, X arrived, sweaty and disheveled. "Sorry, but I missed my exit," X explained. "Before we start, can I use the restroom?" With only forty-five minutes left for our interview session, I skipped right to asking questions about why they thought they were the best person for this job.

"Well, I really need this job. I will work really hard to do whatever it takes to do a great job. I'm reliable, responsible, very organized, and I get along great with everybody. If you give me this opportunity, I will not let you down," X explained.

I asked if X had any questions for me. "Well," X began, "what exactly do you do here? I've heard about this company, but I don't know that much about what the business does. Can you fill me in?"

After I gave a brief history of the company from information available on our website, I asked if there was anything else X would like to know. X did not have any questions for me about the open position. The interview ended early. X thanked me for my time and left.

Candidate Y

Y arrived fifteen minutes early for the interview and exchanged a few friendly and polite words with the receptionist. She was shown into my office wearing a big smile and a neatly put together business outfit. Y opened by thanking me for making time to speak with them today. Y went on to say they have read and heard very positive things about my company and were eager to learn more about what the company needs from this new position. "I've read the job description, but it would be really helpful to hear from you what are the most important aspects of this position? What skills would someone need to be successful?"

Y opened a notebook and took brief notes while I talked, listening carefully and maintaining eye contact. When I finished talking, Y then went point by point listing the precise experience they had and the results they were able to accomplish in similar situations. I asked a few clarifying questions which Y answered thoughtfully, not as if they were reciting from a script.

At the end of our hour, Y surprised me by asking if I had any further questions. "Are there any things missing from my qualifications that you feel would disqualify me for this job?"

When I said I thought I had all the information I needed, Y said, "I'm very enthusiastic about this opportunity and feel I would bring real value to the team. What next steps might we take to enable you to choose me?"

Candidate Z

Z showed up on time for their interview, wearing a nice shirt, no jacket, designer jeans, and squeaky clean sneakers. As soon as Z entered my office, they pulled their cell phone out of their pocket and put it, face up, on the desk in front of them. Although it was silenced, notifications kept popping up on the screen. Z quickly glanced over at each notification but was able to keep talking.

Z started by reciting the information on their résumé, listing in order all their job titles and responsibilities. This took about twenty minutes, during which they talked without stopping. When I was finally able to speak, I asked about a specific skill. Z said, "It's on my résumé" and did not elaborate further. When I asked about how Z would handle a specific situation, they said, "I'd have to think about that."

As the interview wrapped up, I asked Z if they had any questions for me. "Not really," Z said, "I'm good."

For every hiring manager I have worked with in my more than thirty-five years in the business, this is an easy decision. All other things being roughly equal, Candidate Y will get the job offer *every single time*. Why? For the obvious reasons. They came prepared. They had done their research about the company. They asked the hiring manager to tell them *specifically* what they were looking for. And the candidate was able, by referencing their experience and skills, to provide concrete examples of *why* they were a perfect fit for the job. But the clincher was what they did in the final moments of the interview. They used a *closing technique*, virtually guaranteed to at least let you know where you stand in the process and ideally remove any obstacles between you and the job offer. This is a basic concept, but it resonates regardless of the role you are interviewing for. These examples of X, Y, and Z's interviews are taken from actual feedback clients have given me about their experiences interviewing prospects. Surprisingly, I have also had candidates interviewing for CEO roles that did not prepare and presented themselves very poorly.

This is a lot to take in, but I want you to review *exactly* what Candidate Y did. Is there anything in the description of the interview that you are not capable of doing? No. There isn't.

My job as an executive search consultant is to make sure you ace the interview because that is the ultimate test. As any competitor will tell you, it doesn't matter what the competition is—sports, dance, video gaming, big game fishing—*you can't win if you are not fully, completely, totally prepared*. And I use the same approach to preparation whether the position someone is interviewing for is entry-level, mid-level, or C suite.

This chapter is about coaching you to crush the interview. You have already done much of the necessary preparation in your work from chapters 1–4. Now, I'm going to share the insider tips that will enable you to ace your interviews and land the job that gets you closer to your Buffalo. If you're going to compete, you need to win!

Unseen Competition

All desirable job opportunities create intense competition, even more so with Internet access to job postings and the potential for "work from anywhere" positions. If you want a particular job, there are bound to be hundreds, even thousands of others who also want the offer. Remember what I said before: the hiring manager is looking for a reason *not* to hire you. They have tons of people who have to be eliminated from the search process. Let's focus your efforts on what it takes to beat the competition. In this case, "winning" means getting the job offer. Anything less is failure.

No Substitutes for Preparation

Hundreds of years ago, Benjamin Franklin said, "By failing to prepare, you are preparing to fail." True then, still true today. Much more recently, Oprah Winfrey said, "I believe luck is preparation meeting opportunity. If you hadn't been prepared when the opportunity came along, you wouldn't have been lucky." You have already completed much of the initial work that will help you stand out. If you have been dedicating time and effort to reach out through informational phone calls and exploration of potential openings, you should begin to receive invitations to interview.

Preparation is key to competitive interviewing. Spending the time and thought it takes to show up informed and ready to showcase your value shows the hiring manager you are *already invested* in their company and this position. Having a clear and easy-to-communicate *why* document will be your most powerful sales tool. Later in this chapter, we'll go deeper into how and when to use your *why* document. But first let's assemble the basics for interview preparation and tracking.

Staying organized is an essential part of the job search process. Ideally, you will have multiple opportunities you are pursuing and potentially multiple offers to consider. Using a simple checklist like this one will enable you to manage the process stress-free.

Interview Preparation Checklist

Interview for (position)
Date:
Time:
Title:
Client Company:
Hiring Manager:

General Concerns

- Review the interview date, time, location, directions, and walk-in instructions.
- Assess the hiring process and research the people whom you are meeting via the web or personal contacts.
- Seek out a mentor/contact who knows the interviewers. Ask what to expect from each interviewer, the types of questions to they are likely to ask, what if any areas of common interest you might have with them.
- Review the company's goals in relation to your expectations.
- Review your concerns about the company and opportunity.
- Review how your experience meets and/or exceeds the specifications of the position in relation to:
  - Duties and Responsibilities
  - Skills, Abilities, and Experience
  - Industry, Product, and Network Knowledge
  - Educational Qualifications
  - Organizational Structure
  - Working Environment
  - Opportunity for Challenge/Advancement
- Ask why the position is open and information about the last person who held the position.
- Review how you will respond to the "tell me about yourself" question.
- Review your response to tough questions or problem areas like:
  - Not having enough/right experience
  - Job hopping
  - Not meeting goals
- Prepare a list of questions to ask the interviewer about the company, responsibilities, expectations, culture, and the manager you would report to.
- Verify your current compensation package.
- Prepare a response to compensation and benefit issues.

- Organize a closing statement asking for the next step/ decision.
- Consider "If this interview meets my expectations, am I prepared to accept an offer at XXX today?"

Personal Readiness

- What to bring:
  - Copies of résumés for each interviewer
  - List of references
  - Notepad and pens in a portfolio
- What to wear:
  - Business attire—pressed, polished, and subdued, appropriate to employer standards and relevant to the position, for instance a construction job vs. a sales associate role. *Dress for the job you want.*
  - Check body, hair, jewelry, and perfume for distractions
  - Remember the importance of body language
- What to do:
  - Arrive ten minutes early (or perhaps pre-trip the day before especially if relocation or unfamiliar area)
  - Acknowledge assistant or staff on site and treat with respect
  - Turn off and store cell phone
  - Transmit positive energy—let your personality show
- What *not* to do:
  - Eat, drink, smoke before interview
  - Drink alcohol during lunch/dinner interview
  - Speak negatively about prior employers
  - Discuss compensation, benefits, vacation too early in the process
  - Linger after the interview or discuss the job while walking around the client's building

Interview Debrief Checklist

Remember you are a *job hunter*, actively looking for the *best* opportunity, your true Buffalo. You are not a passive seeker desperately hoping for someone, anyone to hire you. This is a very important mind shift for most people. Confidence is important. They are going to interview you for a fit, but you must also interview them. It is not about who will hire you but who is going to be lucky enough to have you join their team and bring your skills, experience, and talent to help them achieve their goals. In each interview, you should be evaluating the company to determine if they are a good fit for you. This checklist offers some prompts to help you weigh your options.

Client Company:

Interviewer:

Interview Number (initial, or follow-up interview):

Date of Interview:

- How did my interview go? How long was I there?
- Who did I meet with? How did I relate to the people I met? Can I see myself working for/with these people?
- Was I introduced to anyone else? Who? Title?
- How did they describe the position to me?
- What are the positive points I recognized about the position?
- Were there any differences in what was described and what I thought the position included?
- Can I do the job? Do I *want* the job?
- What do I think about the company?
- What do I think about the career growth potential for this position and company?
- What are the negatives that concern me about the position or company?
- What is my interest level on a 1 to 10 scale, with 10 being the greatest level of interest? What would make it a 10?

- Did I discuss compensation at an appropriate time?
- Did I discuss any benefits when relevant?
- How does this position compare with any other positions for which I am interviewing?
- How did the interview end? Did I ask for the next step/another interview?
- If an offer came through tomorrow, what would I need to know in order to accept it?
- Is there anything preventing me from resigning/accepting the position tomorrow?
- Are there any personal considerations that need to be taken into account? (Family, home, bonus, benefits, et cetera)

The *Why* Document—A Recruiter's Secret Weapon

After you've done the basic preparation and are ready to track the results, investing time in completing what I call the *why* document is going to give you a competitive edge over other candidates. Once again, you've already done most of the work that will enable you to build a powerful *why* document. You know what you value most in a position, you know your strengths and abilities, you've described measurable results you've been able to achieve, and you've done research on your target companies.

Take a look at this sample *why* document to see how to build your own.

Sample

Position/Opportunity: VP of Marketing

Problem company is trying to solve:
- Increase online presence with the goal of increasing online generated sales.

Describe in measurable ways how you would benefit the employer:

- I have twenty years of experience in online digital marketing. Over the past eight years, I have led a team of fifteen marketing coordinators whose goal was to develop a positive online presence for the company and generate online sales revenue.

Acknowledge employer successes and identify how you would add to them:

- Currently your online platform has great promise. With my knowledge and expertise in this vertical, I will be able to turn online viewers into online customers.

Highlight your most valuable skills and accomplishments:

- In the last two years, the online marketing campaigns I have created and managed have increased revenues 30 percent year over year. I will bring this knowledge and motivation to your company to achieve the increase in the online sales market that the company is looking for.

Now use this template to build your own *why* document for any opportunity you are exploring.

Position/Opportunity:

_____

_____

Problem company is trying to solve:

_____

_____

Describe how you'd benefit the employer:

_____

_____

Acknowledge employer successes and identify how you'd add to them:

_____

_____

Highlight your most valuable skills and accomplishments:

_____

_____

Using the questions below, take a moment to review your practice *why* document. Does it answer these essential questions? Your goal is to tell employers in no uncertain terms what value you bring to the company. You want to provide clear and persuasive reasons why they should hire *you*.

Is my *why* document specific and to the point?

_____

_____

Do you explain your two or three most relevant skills and suggest how they would impact the employer? Do you offer specific examples of your impact?

_____

_____

Do you speak to the employers' successes and challenges, and how you can address them?

_____

The Interview in Four Acts with Three Goals

I've said every interview is a brutal competition, but I'm going to change metaphors. You can also think about interviews like a play or story with four parts: Beginning, Middle, Close, and Afterword. Along the way, there are three main goals you need to accomplish. As you move through this process, you have the opportunity to do something memorable and powerful. Don't waste it.

The Beginning

The opening minutes count. As the saying goes, you only make one first impression, so be sure to enter wearing a genuine smile and radiating positive energy. Offer a firm handshake and make solid eye contact. Be sure to thank the person for taking this time to meet with you. Take a seat and be mindful of your body language—avoid squirming, slouching, looking around, or other distracting movements.

Every good interview is a dialogue, a conversation in which both people take turns talking and listening. In fact, a good target to aim for is to allow the hiring manager to do at least 55 percent of the talking, leaving 45 percent of the airtime for you. Your first goal is to encourage the hiring manager to share pertinent information with you.

A strong opening move is to get the hiring authority to tell you *exactly* what they are looking to hire for. You want to reassure them that you've read the job description, but you'd like to hear from them what they think being successful in the job requires. It's generally a good strategy to ask the interviewer about themselves—not personal information but about their experience working for the company, what made them choose a career here, and what they like about the organization. You can also ask for their insights about challenges their industry is facing and specific problems their company is trying to solve. What do they think the future holds for the company?

As Candidate Y did, take brief notes of any key phrases or words you hear. These will form the basis for how you describe yourself as you are formulating your specific *why* document for this position.

This is goal one—get the hiring authority to tell you exactly what they are looking for.

The Middle

After carefully listening, it's now your time to talk. This is when you pull out your secret weapon: your customized *why* document. The middle of an interview is the time when you sell yourself as the best possible candidate.

Unfortunately, many people have a negative association with the idea of sales, but in reality, we are all salespeople, especially in an interview situation. A good salesperson never starts a pitch without knowing what the customer (the hiring manager) needs and wants to buy. If you're applying for a chef's job at a vegan restaurant, you're not going to brag about your extensive recipes for cooking with beef, pork, and cheese. That's not what's going to land you the gig.

Don't start selling yourself until you know what the prospect *values*. Building on the care you took writing a *why* document to prepare for this interview, you can now tailor your presentation to what the interviewer has just told you. You should speak *directly* to what they said they are looking for. Be specific about your skills and track record, being sure to back up every claim with details and examples. You can also think about this as your SAVE reply. In response to hearing a client's need or pain point, your response should contain this information:

S—state that you have the skill to address the problem.
A—cite specific accomplishments from your work history.
V—describe the value you bring to the organization.
E—provide examples of how you have added value in your previous roles.

Through the entire middle portion of your interview, the idea you are selling is *why I am the right candidate for this job*. Period.

This is Goal Two—sell yourself specifically to the hiring authority's stated needs.

You've Got the Mic—Don't Abuse It
One day I got a call from a client to whom I'd sent a potential candidate. I knew the interview was supposed to be that day, so when the client's name popped up on my phone, I thought something must have gone wrong. "Hi, Ron, I'm surprised to get a call. Did my candidate fail to show up for his interview this morning?"

I asked. "No, he's on my other line right now," he replied. "Okay, so I'm not sure what your call is about. What's wrong?" I asked. "I'll tell you what's wrong," he said, "He hasn't stopped talking about himself for over twenty minutes. He's doing a data dump of his entire career. Hold on, I'll put him on speaker so you can hear for yourself. I can't get a word in edgewise." My candidate was selling before he knew what the client was buying. He didn't make it past the first round of interviews.

Another client called to report on her interview with a highly qualified candidate. "I'll be honest, Tom," she confided, "before the interview I was all set to make her an offer. But during the interview, all she kept talking about was her cat—how adorable it was, how much she loved it, what good care she took of it. That might be great if we were a pet care or pet food company but we're a major financial investment firm. Cats don't cut it here." That was the end of the road for the cat lover.

When writing your résumé, my advice is to be 100 percent honest; the same applies to your interview. A little exaggeration is okay, and certainly you don't want to undersell yourself by being too modest, but stick to the truth. Being truthful is not the same as blurting out all your future plans. One of my candidates felt that his interview was going so well that he could confide in the hiring manager. He said, "What I really want to do is start my own business someday." Red flag. The client went from enthusiastic to stone cold, imagining how the company would invest in training and developing this young talent, only to have him become a competitor. Game over. Interview done.

In addition to your *why* document, for more senior positions coming prepared with a high-level business plan is powerful. It may be as simple as a professionally printed outline suggesting what you feel needs to be done in your first thirty, sixty, or ninety days on the job. Or it could be as elaborate as a brief PowerPoint presentation on your laptop laying out a six-month or one-year plan. In a few slides, you could identify the key challenges, ask intelligent questions about what you couldn't possibly know, and suggest approaches or recommendations as possible solutions. Unless you are wildly off the mark in your analysis and strategy, most hiring managers will be very impressed by your business sense and professionalism.

The Close

How are you feeling as your interview wraps up? Excited by what you've learned? Enthusiastic about the company and the culture? Convinced that this is your Buffalo? Or none of the above? That's okay too because, remember, you are interviewing the company to test for a good fit. But if you really want the job, use this powerful tactic I call the Close. This is what I have told every candidate I have ever placed. Feel free to use these exact words or modify them to suit your personality!

"Thank you very much for the time you've spent with me today. The more I learn about the position and the company, the more excited I am. Based on what you've shared, I believe I'd be a great addition to the team. I'd really like to move forward." Then ask (and here's the most important part), "Do you have any concerns or questions about me that would prevent you from moving me forward?"

Now, be quiet and listen. This is a yes or no decision. You are putting them on the spot so that you have a chance to overcome any objections they might still have. If they have a question or concern, you need to hear it so you can address it and offer more information. They will either let you down or move you along. If they say, "Yes, I have some concerns," get them to tell you what they are. Perhaps they missed something in your background, education, or experience that they feel is necessary. Maybe you can fill in that gap and stay in the running. Or maybe knowing it's a liability, you will address this before you go for any other interviews.

If they say "No, I don't have more concerns," then ask, "What is the next step in the process?" Try to get a commitment of some sort for a next interview, a tour of the facility, paperwork, whatever it might be. Getting a definite next step means you are that much closer to getting an offer. Most candidates don't do any of this, and that's a costly mistake. Getting the hiring manager to make a decision while you're there leaves you in a much stronger position. Instead of being kept in the dark you have a much better idea of where things stand. By the way, this process works regardless of the type of interview—phone, video, or in person.

A word about discussing compensation: it is usually not a good idea to start off an interview with demands about salary, benefits, and vacation. However, when the interviewer brings up the topic, and sooner or later they will, be prepared to respond. The most effective negotiating tactic I've used successfully is to keep your options open. You can candidly tell them what your current compensation package is with benefits included. I've found that if you are honest about your current level but let the interviewer know you are "open to any offer," you've set the bar but haven't ruled anything out. You're certainly not going to accept an offer before you fully understand the compensation package. Just don't make this an obstacle that may stop you from being fully considered and valued as a viable candidate.

As with every other piece of information you have shared about yourself, you are trying to get them to realize you are the right, the best, the must-have person for the job.

This is Goal Three, CLOSE!

Here are a few examples of common scenarios to help you design your own approach. You'll find more variations described in the Appendix.

Interview Closing Techniques

a) Alternate Close/Alternative Choice
    This close gives the individual a choice between two positives.
    Choosing either one confirms a decision.

    Example:
    "Let's compare calendars. Is Wednesday the 7th or Thursday the 8th a good time to continue our discussion?

b) Ben Franklin/Balance Sheet
The balance sheet close creates a visual. List all the positive reasons why you are a good fit for the position. Simply listen as the person lists or tries to come up with negatives or explain that there aren't any negatives.

Example:
"Let me explain why I believe I am a fit for your company/ position. Please take out a blank piece of paper and draw a line down the center—like a T account. On the left, I'm going to describe all the reasons how I fit the opportunity and, on the right, identify the reasons how I do not fit."

c) Puppy Dog/Trial Close
Drop off the "puppy" and let them keep him for a short period without making an upfront payment/commitment.

Example:
"I understand you do not have a full-time position available now. What if I was to work on an interim basis where you would only pay for the hours I worked, where you could take a sample, in other words? If I perform well, you will consider converting my role to a full-time position. You really can't lose. Is that reasonable?" I call this a *working interview*.

d) Reduce to Ridiculous
This close allows you to reduce a money concern to its lowest amount for you and the client.

Example:
"I was hoping you would present an offer $2,000 higher. If you take a look at how that $2,000 difference would impact your company, you are talking about $5.47 a day. If you figure in taxes, the difference is really under $3 a day. However, I have

bills that have to be met and need the $2,000. Are you willing to walk away from the perfect candidate over a small difference?"

e) Sharp Angle/Right Angle/Condition
When using this close, you are responding to a statement with a question. This question isolates a given situation and tests if it is preventing the individual from making a decision.

Example:
(Hiring Authority): "I like your experience, but I wish you had a CFA designation."
(Your response): "So if I did have a CFA, you would be ready to move forward?"

f) Summary Close
Simply reiterate their needs and wants, and how you satisfy those needs and wants.

Example:
"From what you said before, you were looking for ten plus years' experience, a business degree, project management skills, implementation experience, and utilizing multi-platform architecture. Is that right? I am on target in all categories. Don't you agree?"

The Afterword

No matter how well or how terrible you think the interview went, you absolutely must send a thank-you note to the interviewer. An email is acceptable if you send it the same day. But now when email inboxes are always overstuffed, also following up the next day with a clean handwritten note on nice stationery is much more likely to impress. Keep it simple, sincere, and professional. Something like one of these examples would be fine.

Dear [Interviewer Name], Thank you so much for meeting with me this week. It was such a pleasure to learn more about the team and position, and I'm very excited about the opportunity to join [Company Name] and help [bring in new clients/develop world-class content/anything else awesome you would be doing] with your team. I look forward to hearing from you about the next steps in the hiring process, and please do not hesitate to contact me if I can provide additional information.

Sincerely,
[your name]

Dear Ms. Smith: Thank you for taking the time out of your busy schedule to meet with me about the senior programmer analyst position with Acme Office Supplies. I appreciate your time and consideration in interviewing me for this position. After speaking with you and the group, I believe that I would be a perfect candidate for this position, offering the quick learning and adaptability that is needed for a diversified position. In addition to my enthusiasm for performing well, I would bring the technical and analytical skills necessary to get the job done. I am very interested in working for you and look forward to hearing from you once the final decisions are made regarding this position. Please feel free to contact me at any time if further information is needed. Thank you again for your time and consideration.

Sincerely,
[your name]

(More detailed) Dear Name: It was a pleasure to meet you after our many emails and phone conversations regarding the Production Editor / Proofreader position. I truly enjoyed hearing about the Management Group and learning more about the needs of the Sales Intelligence Department. I appreciated being able to share some of the reasons why I feel that I am the ideal candidate for the job. I also appreciated touring your facilities. They are quite impressive, and it would be a true joy to work in such beautiful surroundings.

Thank you also for introducing me to several members of your sales intelligence team. They were all so kind and accommodating. Please let them know I appreciate how comfortable they made me feel. I agree it was unfortunate that Bob Brown, the actual person to whom I'd report, was not in the office. I hope he is feeling better, and I look forward to coming back to meet with him when it's convenient. After talking with you, meeting the team, and getting a better understanding of what is involved in the position, I am even more confident that there can be no better match. Don Pearce showed me several recent projects, and Jody Fryer explained the process and gave me a look at the computer applications that I might be using. I am very familiar with the entire setup and have done work almost identical to the examples that I was shown.

Currently, my schedule is flexible, and knowing your urgency to fill the position, I would like to meet Mr. Brown at his earliest convenience. Please drop me an email or a quick call with a date and time, and I'll be sure to arrange my schedule so that I can meet Mr. Brown. Thank you again for your time; I look forward to hearing from you soon.

Sincerely,
[Your name]

One final thought about "afterward." Sometimes you don't get the job and someone else does. But for whatever reason, thirty, sixty, or ninety days later it hasn't worked out and the position is open again. If it's a job you really want, don't hesitate to reach out to the hiring manager at one or more of these intervals with a friendly "touching base" kind of email. "I am following up to see if perhaps there are any new opportunities that may be a good fit for my skills and experience." If something has happened with the person they hired and you were the second-choice candidate, reaching out to the manager can put you at the top of the list, especially when you are gracious about not having been their first choice. Stay positive, no matter what.

As you move toward a decision—and remember the goal of this process is to get to a decision—and they offer you the role, that is a win.

The three goals apply to every round of the interviewing process; just go deeper and into more detail with each successive round of interviews.

One of my best techniques to insure my candidates get an offer is to prepare a 30—60—90—180—360 high-level business plan. Imagine that during the final interview, they offer you a blank sheet of paper and ask you to outline your plans for the first year. You may not have enough information to do a detailed plan, but you should have enough to share your thoughts, suggestions, and questions. It should be just a few pages, well prepared. It is an example of your work product, leadership style, etc.

What Is the Point of an Interview Anyway?

Some final aspects of the interview process to consider are the various styles of interviews and the characteristic types of questions you are likely to encounter. It can't be overstated that in the competitive market of job interviews, the hiring manage is trying to minimize the risk to the company. Their overall goal in hiring is to seek employees who:

- Display enthusiasm for the company, its business, and its people.
- Believe that s/he can do the job and has well matched skills.
- Are coachable and strive to make an immediate contribution.

Employers also factor in personal chemistry, personality match, experience, relocation, salary expectations, solid references, et cetera to determine a person's qualifications and suitability for employment. Yet, they seek more than that. The "more" consists of thirteen predictive skills and behaviors that employers evaluate through behavioral-based interviewing techniques in order to make solid hiring decisions. These traits are described in more detail below.

Interviews must be professional conversations during which both parties willingly exchange information that allows them to arrive at a sound, mutual commitment and decision.

Remember: all the right skill sets, achievements, realistic expectations, cooperation, and respect are irrelevant if the person is not truly motivated to make a change!

In order to uncover the motivators and attributes of an individual, an interviewer will often resort to asking four basic types of questions:

- **Fact-finding questions** to verify stated information such as what is on a person's résumé.
- **Technical questions** to assess a person's job-related expertise.
- **Hypothetical questions** to predict performance by asking the person to imagine how s/he might respond to "what if" questions that relate to a possible future situation.
- **Behavioral-based questions** to evaluate a person's potential effectiveness in a new position by asking him/her to share past experiences that are relevant to the new opportunity.

Proponents of the behavioral interview approach contend that past performance is the best predictor of future performance (have done this before, will be able to repeat in the future). In fact, behavioral interviewing is said to be 55 percent predictive of future on the job behavior, while factual interviewing is only 10 percent predictive. More and more companies are using the behavioral approach for this reason. You may even have had interviews that have been behavioral based and if so you will recognize the example questions below. If you haven't been through a behavioral interview, these examples can help you prepare for one.

Behaviors are actions or reactions to a situation. To function effectively in the work environment, an individual must demonstrate appropriate behaviors in three areas—skills, motivation, and "fit" or emotional quotient (EQ)—all of which must be considered during the interview process. Companies can discuss and specifically test for skills, but it is much more difficult to test for motivation and fit.

Behavioral questions are a means to evaluate motivation and fit by linking past or current work-based behaviors to required behavior in an organization. This type of questioning generally begins with "Tell me a time when . . ." or "Describe a situation . . ."

Examples are as follows:

- Give me an example of a time when you set a goal and were able to meet or achieve it.
- Tell me about a time when you were satisfied with your own performance.
- Give me a situation where your persistence paid off.
- Tell me about a time when you had too many things to do, and you were required to set priorities.
- Describe a situation where you failed to reach a goal. How did that affect you?
- Tell me about a time when you had to go above and beyond the call of duty in order to get a job done.
- Give me an example of a time when you showed initiative and took the lead.

These questions are intended to provide insight into your relationships with superiors and subordinates, projects, and tasks (both positive and negative), and other relevant work experience.

While there are no right or wrong answers, there is a most effective way to respond to behavioral-based questions. We refer to this as the STAR method. This approach is a tool that psychologists and criminal/legal specialists have used for many years to uncover motives.

When used effectively, it enables interviewers to hear your explanation of why an action was taken, how you dealt with the action, and what resulted from it.

The STAR approach stands for:

S—describe the **situation.**
T—describe the specific **task.**
A—explain what **action** was taken.
R—describe the outcome or **result** of your actions.

Commonly the interviewer will set up a scenario and then ask you to respond with how you have reacted in the past. Give an example of a **situation** in which you were involved that resulted in a positive or negative outcome. Describe the **tasks** involved in that situation. List the actions or behaviors demonstrated, specifics, and how it was accomplished. (This is where behavioral traits are uncovered). Talk about the various **actions** involved in the situation's tasks. Describe specific actions that were taken or not taken, using "I" or "we." Detail the result—a specific, tangible conclusion that completes the picture. What **results** followed because of your actions?

Conclude each story using specific, measurable terms.

To illustrate how the STAR process might be followed, assume that a hiring authority asked an individual to provide an example that demonstrates why the candidate believes he is a good manager. A thoughtful candidate using the STAR method would reply like this:

Situation:

"Relocation expenses in the company were out of control and quickly exceeding the budget . . ."

Task:

"When I took on this responsibility . . ."

Action:

"I focused on reviewing the reports and working with tenured staff to determine key entry points to maximize efforts and contain specific expenses. The staff assisted me by making a series of cost-effective recommendations and together we drafted a plan."

Result:

"We then jointly developed a workflow system to maximize the effectiveness of the new procedure that became the company standard and is still in place and maintained."

Such pre-interview preparation is time well spent as it offers you an opportunity to view your experience from a different perspective, one that you probably have not previously considered.

Below are key reminders of what occurs while in a behavioral-based interview:

Remember that during a behavioral interview, employers are attempting to highlight the skills necessary for the job and then asking focused questions to assess whether the candidate possesses those skills. Make it a point to read company literature or websites carefully and listen closely during the company's information session to determine which skills an employer is seeking. You only want to "sell" what the client wants to "buy."

Here is a typical list of the skills and behaviors interviewers will be screening for followed by the sorts of questions they are likely to pose:

1. Focus and dedication to the industry
   Does the person's résumé reflect enough experience, knowledge, and growth in a chosen field?
   - Specifically, what attracts you to this industry as a career?
   - Why did you choose your major or career?
   - At what point did you make this decision?

2. Technical and professional knowledge
   Does the person have an appropriate level of understanding of technical skills, professional knowledge, and the ability to apply both?
   - Tell me about a time when you had a customer say "no" to you when selling (a product).

3. Teamwork
   Does the person work effectively with others in the organization and outside the formal lines of authority (i.e., peers, other departments, senior management) to accomplish organizational goals and to identify and resolve problems? Does s/he consider the impact of his/her decision on others?
   - Describe for me a situation where others you were working with on a project disagreed with your ideas. What did you do?

4. Analysis

   Is the person able to relate and compare data from different sources, identify issues, secure relevant information, and determine relationships?

   - Describe a situation when you had to determine the most pertinent content for your sales presentation.

5. Adaptability

   Does the person maintain effectiveness in varying environments, tasks, and responsibilities, and with various types of people?

   - Tell me about a situation when you had to work with other departments to solve a common problem.

6. Work Standards

   Has the person set high goals or performance standards for him/herself, subordinates, others, and the organization? Is s/he dissatisfied with average performance?

   - Tell me how you measure your performance. How do you set goals for yourself in your current role?
   - How have you differed from your manager in evaluating your performance? How did you handle the situation?

7. Job Motivation

   To what extent do activities and responsibilities available in the job overlap with activities and responsibilities that result in personal satisfaction?

   - Give examples of what causes you to feel dissatisfied in your job and why.
   - Give examples of what provides you with job satisfaction and why.
   - Describe the type of manager with which you do your best work. Why?

8. Initiative
   Does the person make active attempts to influence events and achieve goals? Is s/he self-starting rather than passively accepting? Does s/he go beyond what is necessary?
   - Describe a situation that required a number of tasks to be done at the same time.
   - How did you handle it? What was the result?
   - Describe a project that was implemented or successfully carried out primarily due to your efforts.
   - Have you found any ways to make your job easier or more rewarding? Describe them.

9. Ability to learn
   Does the person assimilate and apply new job-related information promptly?
   - What techniques have you learned to make your job easier or more effective? How did you learn them?
   - Tell me about a time when you had to quickly assimilate new information to solve a problem or perform well in your current role.

10. Planning and organizing
    Does the person establish a course of action to accomplish specific goals? Does s/he plan proper assignments for personnel and allocate resources appropriately?
    - How do you determine priorities in scheduling your time?
    - Describe a time when numerous projects were due at the same time. What steps did you take to complete your tasks?

11. Communication
    Does the person clearly express ideas in speaking and writing, via his/her grammar, organization, and structure?
    - What has been your experience in giving presentations to small or large groups?

- What has been your most successful experience in either situation?
- Tell me about a time when your listening skills really paid off, perhaps a time when other people missed the key idea being expressed by the speaker.
- Describe how you know you've presented information effectively.

12. Customer service orientation
    Does the person make efforts to listen to and understand the customer (both internal and external), anticipate customer needs, and give high priority to customer satisfaction?
- Tell me about the most difficult customer service experience you have handled, perhaps with an angry or irate customer. Be specific, discuss what you did, and explain the outcome.

13. Sensitivity
    Does the person act out of consideration for the feelings and needs of others?
- Describe a situation in which you found yourself dealing with someone who didn't like you. How did you handle that?
- Give an example of when you had to work with someone who was difficult to get along with. How did you handle that?

Additional behavioral questions:

- Give an example of a time in which you felt you were able to build motivation in your coworkers or subordinates at work.
- Has anyone ever asked you to do something unethical? What did you do?
- Tell me about your role in a project team. What did you do to contribute toward a team environment? Be specific.

- Describe the most creative work-related project you have carried out.
- Describe a work situation in which you had to take a risk. What was the outcome?
- Tell me about a time when you delegated a project effectively.
- Give me an example of a time when you motivated others.
- Describe a situation when you needed to get an understanding of another's viewpoint before you could get your job done. What problems did you encounter and how did you handle them?
- Describe a situation when you had a personal commitment that conflicted with an emergency business meeting. What did you do?
- Have you ever had to make an unpopular decision/announcement? Describe how you handled it.
- Tell me about a time when you had to work with someone you found difficult.
- What made that person difficult? How did you handle it?
- Describe a time when you set your sights too high (or too low).
- Describe a time when you anticipated potential problems and developed preventive measures.
- Tell me about a time when you missed an obvious solution to a problem.
- Give an example of a time when you tried to accomplish something and failed.
- Tell me about a difficult decision you've made in the last year.
- What is your typical way of dealing with conflict? Give an example.
- Give an example of a time when you had to make a split-second decision.
- Give a specific example of a time when you had to conform to a policy with which you did not agree.

- Tell me about a time when you had to use your presentation skills to influence someone's opinion.
- Give me a specific example of a time when you used good judgment and logic in solving a problem.
- Describe a time when you were faced with a stressful situation that demonstrated your coping skills.

The best way to handle behavioral questions is to practice your answers in advance. Run through this list of questions before you face an interviewer and have situations, tasks, actions, and positive results ready to go. You will find this saves you the embarrassment of not being able to come up with an answer on the spot or perhaps even worse, protects you from offering an example that does not put you in the best light. As you gain more interviewing experience, you will find that certain questions are favorites of interviewers. Pay attention to the response your answers are getting and continue to refine and polish your replies. That's the most reliable way to ace any behavioral interviews.

Final Words of Advice

As you go through the application process, chances are you will be asked to interview in various ways—by phone, over videoconference, or in person. While the method may vary, there is some advice that remains constant:

Be prepared.

Be professional.

Look your best. Find out what the dress code is and go one step further. It is always better to be overdressed than underdressed.

Be conversational. Don't do more than 45 percent of the talking.

Be ready with probing and thoughtful questions.

Never talk negatively about your previous employer.

Have your SAVE and *why* document customized for each interviewer.

Making a Zoom Impression

Tiffany's flagship store in Manhattan asked me to find them some candidates for a prestigious sales position. The applicants needed to be fluent in Mandarin in order to serve the growing Chinese market. Two candidates with virtually identical credentials made it to the semifinal round of Zoom interviews.

Candidate One decided to take the Zoom interview while she was out doing errands. She did not activate her camera, only the audio. At the time, she was in a grocery store in Chinatown where there was a lot of background noise. The client had a hard time hearing her answers and the candidate frequently had to ask the interviewer to repeat their questions. Given the difficult circumstances, the interviewer cut short the interview after fifteen minutes. The hiring manager came away with the distinct impression that the applicant was uninterested in the job.

Candidate Two shared a small apartment with two roommates, both of whom worked from home. Knowing it would be impossible to have a quiet or private conversation from his apartment, Candidate Two looked for another solution. A friend's parents owned a condo overlooking Central Park in Manhattan. Candidate Two arranged to use their living room for an hour while he was on his scheduled Zoom interview. He carefully positioned his laptop facing Central Park so that his video background was a gorgeous view of this famous park. He wore a suit and tie and was impeccably groomed. He was also prepared with answers to typical interview questions. From the first moment of appearing on camera, he impressed the interviewer with his maturity, poise, and professionalism. The interviewer recognized that he had found a good fit for Tiffany.

I'll close this chapter the same way I began, by reminding you that there will be intense competition for every good job. There will be many, many candidates who are qualified "on paper." What will keep you in the running is your level of preparation and attention to detail. If you continue to demonstrate your investment in the opportunity throughout the application process, offer an honest appraisal of your skills and abilities, and make a convincing statement for how you alone will bring the most value to the company, your chances will be vastly improved. Follow the tips and insights from this chapter and you will see what I mean.

At the end of the day, only one person wins. I want it to be you.

CHAPTER 6

Transitioning to Your New Job

Do you see what I see? Right there on the horizon. It's your Buffalo—you are nearly there.

All those hours you sacrificed preparing for your job hunt, the nights and weekends when you could have been hanging out or doing tons of many more fun things than executing on your career management plan have finally paid off. You've got at least one job offer that you are truly excited about. Congratulations! You have earned this, and you deserve it.

Although you can see your Buffalo just ahead, there are still a few obstacles to overcome and some common mistakes to avoid. Your transition to the new position is every bit as important as the steps leading up to it. An accepted offer is not the end of your responsibilities. The transition period of leaving one job and settling into another can easily last for ninety days or more. Changing jobs is an emotional situation that requires coaching and support. In fact, mental health professionals consider job changes to be as stressful as divorce or moving. In this chapter, I'll offer advice and support to help you navigate the perils of counteroffers, manage resignation discussions, share news of your new position with your professional network, and get off to a strong start in your exciting new role.

Avoid the Trap of Counteroffers

Let's start by considering what might happen when you tell your boss you are resigning.

The "I'll Say Anything" Tactic

Jenn was a young associate attorney, bright, ambitious, and frustrated with the slow pace of promotion and advancement she saw in her current firm. It was a deeply conservative, old-boy network company culture and while the firm did excellent legal work, Jenn did not feel her talent was valued enough to enable her to be considered for an eventual partner's role. Quietly she launched a job search and soon received an offer from her first choice, a smaller firm with a tremendous reputation. The partners were committed to growing the diversity of their staff and offered Jenn a partner position in recognition of her training, experience, and commitment. Jenn was delighted to have found her dream job.

When she made an appointment to speak with her current boss, he sensed something might be up. Jenn had made it clear that she wanted to be on the partner track, and she had certainly put in the billable hours to show her dedication. But the other partners did not feel she "had what it took" to make partner.

Jenn had prepared her resignation speech but still felt nervous as she faced her boss, who remained seated behind his huge desk. "Eugene, I want to thank you for everything you've done for me since I started here, but I've come to tell you I am resigning. I've taken a position with another firm and will be joining them in two weeks," Jenn said.

Eugene barely waited for Jenn to stop speaking before he cut in, expressing how deeply disappointed he was and how highly everyone in the firm thought of her. He pressed Jenn to divulge the details of the offer she had accepted. After she finished describing the offer, Eugene said simply, "We can match that. And you are definitely on track to make partner here. We want you to stay."

Jenn didn't know what to say. She had not expected a counteroffer. How could she turn Eugene down when he was making an equal offer? Flustered and confused, Jenn agreed to stay. She called the other firm and said she had changed her mind.

Fast-forward three months. Jenn received a raise and a new title but when the partners voted on her promotion, she was turned down. Unknown to Jenn, immediately after she offered her resignation, her boss started looking for her replacement. "She's ready to leave us," he told the other partners, "so we'd better line up a new hire now."

First let me clarify something significant. When I talk about resignations and counteroffers, I'm *not* talking about those instances when you have received an offer but don't tell your current boss. This also does not include offers that you never intended to take yet you tell your employer about them anyway as a "they want me but I'm staying with you" ploy. Unsolicited offers or offers you have turned down can be astute positioning tactics you may choose to use to reinforce your worth by letting your boss know you have other options even though you have no immediate plans to leave. These ploys can be useful *reminders* to your boss that other employers recognize your value and want to recruit you.

When you notify your boss of a genuine offer that you intend to accept, you are in effect submitting your resignation. It's this situation that will cause the panicked employer to respond with a counteroffer. A counteroffer is an inducement from a current employer to entice the current employee (you) to stay in his/her current position, an offer typically given right after the individual has declared his/her intention to leave. There are two main forms of counteroffers: financial and emotional.

Examples of financial counteroffers are:

- a salary increase
- a one-time bonus
- a promotion or added responsibility
- a promise of future raise
- the creation of a new, more appealing reporting structure or company organization

There may even be tangible nonfinancial perks like a bigger office or a reserved parking spot.

Emotional counteroffers, on the other hand, do not cost the employer anything yet are deliberately calculated to change the employee's mind. They frequently take the form of spoken comments which:

- cause guilt
- evoke positive and pleasant memories of social, business, and personal encounters
- express the boss's personal feelings of loss and disappointment
- demean or disparage the new employer or job
- offer vague future promises that things will "get better"

Counteroffers are given for a variety of reasons, however the primary reason is employee retention. In nearly every situation, keeping a good employee is far more cost-effective for the company than replacing one. Whenever a job opening occurs, companies incur the inconvenience and expense of advertising the new position, vetting candidates, completing a thorough evaluation of the potential hires, negotiating the offer, and closing the deal. Additional costs include lost productivity while the position remains open, then reduced productivity while the new hire goes through onboarding and the training period required to get up to speed. Less measurable but still a cost factor are the accompanying stresses and frustrations felt by other employees during the period the company is shorthanded.

From a management perspective, losing a valuable employee always reflects poorly on the boss. No one wants to have a reputation as being difficult to work for since this will damage their own potential for advancement in the company. A boss who is put on the spot by the resignation of a valuable employee will resort to offering more money or making promises (which may never be fulfilled) in order to "fix" the immediate problem. Meanwhile s/he very commonly starts a discreet search for your replacement in a planned way to enable them to manage a more convenient and less disruptive transition on his/her own timetable, not yours.

As Jenn's true story shows, caving in to a counteroffer is never a good idea or a long-term solution for getting closer to your Buffalo.

Before you convey your resignation to your current employer, I urge you to step away and honestly consider these points:

- Why were you motivated to change jobs in the first place?
- Was it only about money? For most people this answer is *no*.
- What does it say about the way your company values its employees that your requests were only responded to after you stated your intention to quit?
- Is the counteroffer a short-term fix or does it offer long-term growth and gratification? (Remember companies can and do renege on "promises" for the future. All they have to do is say something about how the "conditions" of the industry/market/client base/economy have changed.)
- Is your loyalty to the company now in question?
- Has your relationship with your direct supervisor or higher management been damaged?
- Where is the money coming from for any promised increase? Is it just an acceleration of what would have been your next raise?
- If the counteroffer moves you up a level, when is your next opportunity for advancement?
- Will you be considered for a next promotion or passed over for not being a "team player?"

Counteroffers are one talent-preservation tool companies use to prevent being "left hanging high and dry" by an employee who leaves. In making such an offer, your employer might appear to be doing you a big favor. Don't be deceived, though. You aren't the main beneficiary of an accepted counteroffer. During my forty years monitoring the hiring scene, primarily from the standpoint of the executive recruiting industry, it's been clear that the company reaps the most benefits when employees take counteroffers.

Industry pundits may argue that this is no longer true now that the employment paradigm has shifted and the loyalty contract between employers and employees has been irrevocably changed. Some will argue that employees control their destinies more now than they did a decade or two ago and it's sensible for them to use counteroffers to improve their earnings or careers.

But human nature is unalterable—even as the workplace changes around it. Employers aren't charities. They want to avoid the turmoil of transition that occurs when a key player leaves. They also know that for employees, changing jobs ranks as a major stressor with death, divorce, moving, and life's other undesirable speed bumps. They make counteroffers knowing that employees would rather avoid leaving what is familiar. Staying is more comfortable than quitting and facing the unknown by starting over someplace new.

As one human resources executive told me, "My core belief is 'Better the devil you know than the devil you don't.' We understand that matching the salary, changing the job title, creating a new project, or promises of any kind can tip the balance between going and staying. It is a lot cheaper to keep someone than the expense and aggravation of finding a replacement."

Let's face it. When someone resigns, it's a direct reflection on the boss. Unless you're really incompetent or a constant thorn in the boss's side, he or she might look bad by "allowing" you to go. Their gut reaction of self-preservation is to do what's necessary to keep you from leaving until it's convenient for them. That's human nature, too.

If you accept the counteroffer and stay, you'll always be viewed differently. In essence, by agreeing to stay, you've "blackmailed" your boss. From now on, he or she will consider you a "fidelity risk." You lose your status as a team player. You're no longer viewed as an insider.

Nothing truly changes for the better.

Meanwhile, your reasons for wanting to leave still exist. In almost every case, a counteroffer is a temporary fix—a stalling technique to keep you in your seat until the organization can find a suitable replacement. Ask yourself: the next time I feel underpaid, overworked, or otherwise mistreated, will I have to solicit another offer and threaten to resign again in order to correct it?

Let's not forget about the prospective employer, the one who spent long hours and considerable expense to get you that offer. Presumably, you negotiated in good faith and arrived at a mutually acceptable offer. They are counting on you to join them, and they've turned down other qualified candidates. If you renege on your commitment, you taint your reputation. The business community is much smaller than you may think. Word of your lack of integrity can poison your career for decades. And chances are great that this employer you were ready to join will never consider you for any position ever again.

My experience working across industries and at various levels of management is that well-managed companies are proactive about retaining their employees. They don't rely on the tactic of counteroffers to keep their good performers happy and productive. Instead, they achieve their retention successes by operating with fair, equitable, and transparent policies. When I am recruiting and I connect with someone who is happy and content in their role, I try to make that company my client and simply ask for referrals about others they may know outside their company who might be looking. If everything is going well for employees throughout a company, candidates do not raise their hand or even subtly signal for help finding a new position. I want a company like that as a client, since I know from long experience it is always easier to place talent in a well-run organization.

Finally, think about what might happen if your boss decided to fire you. Would he/she accept a "counteroffer" from you? Of course not. His/her decision would be final, and the conversation would be over. Most employee contracts these days are "at will," which means they can fire you and you can resign at any time. You have done your due diligence and invested significant time, talent, and effort to win the offer for better employment that you now have. It's time to trust your research and your judgment. Don't be swayed by your manager's talk of change or his/her remarks downplaying or demeaning your new position. It was his/her job to keep you motivated and happy to work for the current company. He/she didn't do a good enough job of that. So, fire him/her. Statistics show that if you accept a counteroffer, the probability of voluntarily leaving within six months or being let go within one year is extremely high. Move on.

Plan for a Positive Exit Experience

Since the COVID-19 pandemic caused widespread disruption in the business world, we have all heard a lot about the so-called Great Resignation. Story after story feature people who appeared to have abruptly decided to quit their jobs with no real plan, though most of them seemed to have stashed significant money in the bank. My experience indicates that quitting is almost always a difficult process no matter who you are or what your job entails. Nobody I know ever quit a job without worrying.

After you've been in a job for a while, even one you actively dislike, the predictability of the structure, the environment, and the unvarying expectations can be a trap. Human beings love and crave familiarity. It makes us feel safe. Once you know how long your commute is, and you realize that your boss is a jerk, and you can competently perform all the parts of your job—even the really boring ones—the constancy and routineness of your work life can almost have a calming effect. Uncertainty is what you face when you resign for another opportunity. And it's only natural that uncertainty can cause your anxiety to spike.

Generally, we think anxiety is a bad thing. But often anxiety accompanies making hard decisions, the very decisions that will put you on a better, happier, healthier path. Anxiety comes with making any major life change. It's not anxiety that is the problem. It's when that stress makes us question not only our decision but even our ability to make a sound decision.

Once you get caught in the worry loop of self-doubt, there are two likely outcomes: getting completely paralyzed or making a rash choice just to escape uncertainty.

There is a course of action that can prevent you from falling into paralysis or impulsiveness. It involves preparation, reflection, and acceptance. Go back to the early work you did to define your Buffalo. Why are you making a change? What really matters to you? How have you prioritized the key elements of your work and personal life? How will this new opportunity bring you closer to getting what you want out of life?

You've *prepared* yourself for this moment of resignation by thinking honestly about your Buffalo and doing the work to identify the job you want with the company or enterprise you want to align with. *Reflecting* on what you did to get this offer should help calm your nerves.

There was nothing rash or false in your process. You can still worry about what the new job will be like, but instead of getting cold feet, use the worry to problem solve for how you will make the transition less disruptive and emotionally draining. Reexamining your reasons for leaving reminds you that this is the right decision, even if it feels uncomfortable.

Accepting the difficult nature of change will also drop your anxiety level considerably. Be realistic. Change is hard. You're leaving a place of great "knowns" and going to a place full of "unknowns." Recognize that you're going to be vulnerable, feel awkward, and maybe even experience a bit of "impostor syndrome" as you grow into your new role. Transitions can't be rushed. Be realistic about the time you need to adjust, and don't worry about the things you can't control. Be thoughtful about the things you can control, the parts of your daily life that keep you sane and healthy. Your routine is bound to be somewhat disrupted, but don't lose it altogether. Make a plan to take care of your-self and enlist the support of a loved one or friend who can help you.

Most importantly, avoid dwelling on "what's the worst thing that could happen?" and catastrophizing. Don't let worry change your mind. Stick to your decision and calmly, rationally, and professionally leave your old job behind. Even if you made a mistake, few bad decisions can't be undone.

Going for Greener Grass

Carmen had been steadily moving up the career ladder in a bike-share company he really liked.

His supervisor recognized his talent and always encouraged and acknowledged him. His coworkers felt like a happy family. The company regularly celebrated its successes, giving credit to the staff for their excellent efforts. The only problem was money. As a relatively young company, the bikeshare organization couldn't afford to pay top salaries. While Carmen had previously been content with his earnings, he and his wife were expecting their first child. Suddenly, he felt he needed to get a significant boost in his earnings.

Nights and weekends Carmen started researching potential opportunities based on his experience, education, and the need to remain in his same geographic location. He was methodical and diligent in his approach and after several weeks, he was invited to interview with a national media company whose corporate offices were nearby.

When he arrived for his interview, Carmen was struck by how luxurious the offices were and how conservatively dressed the staff were. People were polite and professional but lacked the warmth and personality of his current employers. After two rounds of interviews, the media company reached out with a very attractive offer and a considerable bump in salary. Carmen felt he couldn't turn it down.

The next day he arranged to meet with his supervisor at the bikeshare company. Carmen started the conversation by reminding his boss that he and his wife were expecting their first baby. "I really like working here, and working with you has been tremendous, but with the additional financial responsibility for a child, I felt I needed to find a position that could offer me more benefits and compensation. I don't want to leave you in an awkward position while you look for my replacement, so I am willing to stay for three weeks to give you more time to fill my spot."

Carmen's boss couldn't hide his disappointment. He had worked with Carmen for a few years and felt proud of how he had helped Carmen mature and grow professionally. Plus, Carmen was well-liked and always a positive team player. He would be hard to replace. "Carmen, I have to admit I am sorry to lose you, but as a dad myself I completely understand. I wish there was something I could do but as you know, we're not in a position to offer raises at this time. I appreciate your offer of three weeks' notice. You're going to be hard to replace, but I know I can count on you to help with the training if we bring in a new person before you leave." It was a hard conversation for Carmen, but he felt good about leaving on friendly, professional terms. And he was getting excited about his new job and bigger paycheck.

After several weeks at his new job with the media company, Carmen was miserable. The company culture was cutthroat, people were totally unhelpful and unfriendly, and all anyone seemed to care about was the "bottom line." Carmen told his wife how unhappy he was, and she suggested he reach out to his former boss. "It can't hurt," she said, "he has always looked out for you and maybe he can give you some good advice." Carmen contacted his old boss later that week, suggesting they meet up for a beer after work. His boss was happy to hear from Carmen. When they met at a popular pub, Carmen didn't hold back about his disappointment in the new job. "I'm making more money but that's the only good thing I can say about it," he admitted. "I wish I'd never left."

Carmen's boss smiled. "Your timing is perfect. We've just acquired another bikeshare program and secured a big contract. We're hiring for new positions at several levels. I'd be happy to sponsor you for a management role on the regional team."

Carmen sailed right into the new job at his old company, making more money and feeling that this was where he belonged – with these people in this company. Things would have gone very differently had he not managed his resignation professionally, honestly, and fairly.

Exit Like a Pro

I've already gone to great lengths to convince you what *not* to do when tendering your resignation; *never* accept a counteroffer after you've thoughtfully and carefully made the decision to accept another position elsewhere. Now here are my tips on what you *should* do.

Always resign in person, face-to-face, in a scheduled, private meeting with your boss. Not by text. Not by Slack or email. As awkward and scary as this is, resign when you are sitting in the same room as your boss. No matter what your industry or your position, it's a small world. You want to preserve your reputation as a mature professional who shows respect for his or her supervisor and for the company by delivering this important and sensitive message in person. Keep your remarks short and simple. There's no need to share all the details about your offer. As I've shown, this can only open you up to counteroffers or disparaging remarks about your decision.

Be sure to express gratitude to your current boss for the experience you've had. No need to overdo this, but you can acknowledge that the work you were able to do here has opened new opportunities and enabled you to advance your career. Being grateful to your employer lets them feel appreciated and can soften their disappointment that you are leaving them.

Never "burn a bridge" by saying or doing anything that reflects negatively on the company or your manager. You never know what might happen down the road, as Carmen saw in the last example. Your previous employer may acquire the competitor you left to work for, or your former boss may be recruited by your new company. Stranger things have happened. Do your best to keep your separation clean, painless, unemotional, and businesslike.

Many companies will conduct an exit interview, intentionally designed to help them understand why talent chooses to leave their organization. This is not an opportunity to vent your frustrations or throw certain people under the bus. You can offer constructive criticism if you have any, but being super negative is not going to be well received and it can be held against you. Be honest and fair. Bring up items the company can address if you see areas for improvement. Do not complain about your coworkers. Remember to talk about the positive aspects of the job or company. And don't explain about your new position in detail. You are not under any obligation to tell the HR department any information about your offer.

Give careful thought to the exit interview before it takes place. Leaving is an important part of your career advancement process. Just as meeting in person with your boss is important, take this exit interview process seriously to enable you to depart the company in a positive, professional manner. Your aim should be to stay upbeat while exiting with grace. Anything less risks permanently closing the door on a future relationship.

Once you have notified your immediate supervisor of your intent to leave, you need to follow up with a formal letter of resignation. Resignation letters should thank your prior company and boss for the opportunity and knowledge you've gained while working there. It is customary to give your current employer a two-week notice prior to your last day at the company, but depending on your situation, this may not be possible. Below are resignation letter templates, one giving a two-week notice and the other waiving the two-week notice. Feel free to use these examples as a starting point, then customize them to suit your particular situation.

Notice of Resignation for [Your Name]
Name:
Title:
Dear....,

Please accept this letter as my formal resignation as [position] for [company] to become effective in two weeks, as of _____.

   I want to take this opportunity to thank you for your time and efforts in my training and advancement during the past _____ years. The support shown by you and the rest of the management team has been deeply appreciated. This decision was not an easy one, and involved many days and hours of thoughtful consideration, particularly with respect to my own plans for my future.

   I leave _____ with gratitude and wish you and your company continued success. Please let me know how to best work with you and the team to transition my role.

Sincerely,

Name
CC: President, Direct Supervisor, Personnel, VP
Enclosures:

Notice of Resignation for (Your Name) Waiving Two Weeks' Notice

Name:
Title:
Dear....,

Please accept this letter as my formal resignation as [position] for [company], to become effective as of _____.

   I want to take this opportunity to thank you for the time and effort you invested in my training and advancement during the past _____ years. The support shown by you and the rest of the management team has been deeply appreciated. This decision was not an easy one, and involved many days and hours of thoughtful consideration, particularly with respect to my own plans for my future. Because of a combination of personal and professional obligations, I would like to start my new opportunity as soon as possible. Therefore, I request that you allow me to resign effective immediately if you can accommodate me. Please let me know how to best work with you and the team to transition my role as soon as possible.

I leave _____ with gratitude and wish you and your company continued success.

Sincerely,

Name
CC: President, Direct Supervisor, Personnel, VP
Enclosures:

Start Spreading the News

Depending on the type of company and the level of your position, your new employer may choose to publicize your move to their organization. Typical channels for this sort of communication range from internal company memos to external newspapers, business publications, or trade journals. Positive press about your career is always welcome, but there is more you can and should do on your own after you change jobs.

Begin by making a list of all the people who have contributed to your success—people who gave you encouragement, advice, opened their network of contacts to you, coached or mentored you. Anyone who has helped you obtain interviews, made meaningful introductions for you, served as a reference—all of these people should share in your success. Start by sincerely thanking each and every one of them and letting them know how pleased you are with your new opportunity. You couldn't have done it without them!

A written acknowledgment like a short note on a nice card is an appropriate and powerful touch. Too often we forget the impact of a heartfelt "thank you." Perhaps one day you can repay the favor and you will certainly want to make that offer. You've been the recipient of other people's generosity. Now that you've landed in a position with perhaps more power, influence, and prestige, be sure to repay that generosity—not just to the people who helped you, but to others seeking assistance with their careers. You'll want to be regarded as a "giver" not a "taker," someone who knows how great a difference an individual can make in another person's life simply by doing "five-minute favors" like introductions. Help whoever you can in whatever way you are able. Being generous and supportive will always come back to you.

To reach a broader audience of people in your network who were not involved in your job hunt, use your social media outlets, primarily LinkedIn, to broadcast the good news. It's a great way to remind your business contacts of your ongoing career advancement. Posting a new position gives people an effortless way to reconnect with you over something positive. Be sure to use it to your best advantage.

A Short Account of a Long Relationship

Not long ago, a CEO I knew from professional circles was involved in an acquisition. After the deal went through, he was given a severance package along with a one-year noncompete clause. He took to calling me from time to time during that year as he thought about his next move. I wasn't officially on retainer with him. These were courtesy calls during which I tried to listen to him and offer some free coaching advice. He told me other recruiters weren't taking his calls because they knew he was limited by the noncompete. Whenever he called me, I always took some time to chat.

One day I got a call from him, sharing the news that he had accepted a terrific senior executive position in Atlanta. He was intent on building out a new management team and he asked me to take on the recruitment contract. I told him I was not an expert in his industry and had never worked in the Atlanta market, so I probably wasn't his best bet. "Tom, you're the only person who took my calls when I was out of work. That shows your dedication, your generous spirit, and your professional standards. That's why I want to hire you. The rest I know you'll be able to figure out," he said.

My point is that you should always take the long view. Don't be focused on what's in it for you now. Building and maintaining relationships are investments you want to continue to make throughout your entire working life.

Starting on the Right Foot

This is it! You've started your new job and you are well on your way to your Buffalo. What should you do to ensure success in this new role you've worked so hard to land? Many years ago, my boss gave me some sound advice that still holds 100 percent true. "Tom," he said, "if you want to get ahead, be the first one in in the morning and the last to leave at night." It became a kind of game between us in a friendly and supportive way. One night we were both still at work trying to solve a tough problem long after the others had left. My boss came into my office and told me I should go home. "I'm not leaving until you do," I said with a smile. "Okay," he said, "let's walk out together."

Show your commitment. Be the first to raise your hand for new assignments. Volunteer to help others. Companies place the greatest value on employees who they can count on, the ones who demonstrate their willingness to cheerfully go the extra mile, who show enthusiastic support for their coworkers and supervisors every day.

Don't come into your new job on Day One determined to tell everyone what they are doing wrong. Not long ago I placed a candidate in a great job with a strong company. When his boss called me a few weeks after the placement I expected to hear great things, but instead the manager was unhappy. "The new guy is everything you told us he'd be—smart, experienced, hardworking. But he is running around telling everyone how messed up their operations are," his boss confided. "We all know we've been running shorthanded and making compromises as a result, but it was an interim plan. I wish he would have come to me so I could explain why things are as they are now, and that we are counting on him to fix things. But that's only going to happen if he wins the respect and confidence of the team, and you don't do that by making them all feel incompetent." Fortunately, his supervisor and I were able to have a confidential conversation with the candidate, encouraging him to drop his "bull in a china shop" approach. He listened, took it all in, and set about changing his behavior by apologizing to all he had criticized. After a rocky start, he went on to have great successes in his new role.

Keep in mind that very often the route to your Buffalo will not necessarily involve constantly changing companies, but in moving up the ranks of your current employer. Promotions might be the shortest and most effective path for you to be on. As you begin your new position, think of it as a long-term investment, not a short-term stepping stone. Every new opportunity has the potential to be your dream job if you have a positive mindset and recognize that managing your career is a lifelong process. Relax and enjoy the journey.

CHAPTER 7

For Those Facing Even
Tougher Challenges

Bias. It's an ugly word with terrible implications, especially for the those trying to find their way to their Buffalo. Lately there has been much more open recognition of the role bias plays in so much of our thinking. That's a good thing. It helps us see that *to be human is to have biases and prejudices.* My goal in this chapter is to address that acknowledging the reality of bias, your own and others', can help you make better decisions that will help avoid disappointment and speed you along as you continue your journey to your own unique Buffalo.

Too Old and Female

Crystal spent twenty-five years working as a marketing professional in the automotive industry. While in her mid-fifties, a downturn in the economy led to downsizing throughout her company, and she unexpectedly found herself unemployed, or as I prefer to say, Crystal became a "free agent."

As she reflected on her next step, Crystal decided she'd prefer to leave the auto industry and apply her skills to a comparable senior executive position in health care. She was earning more than $150,000 plus bonus and expected to transition to a comparable

---

role. She set her sights on the premier health-care providers in her region and began submitting online applications. It had been many years since Crystal had gone through the application process, and the lack of response she received puzzled and hurt her.

She came to me for advice after receiving only two invitations for interviews—phone interviews that did not lead to a second round. Crystal began her explanation by saying, "I guess I am seen as being too old to be hired. Too old and a woman in a field dominated by men. Even though I have tons of experience, no one is willing to take me seriously. It doesn't help that the hiring managers are all younger than me."

"Well, Crystal, here's the hard truth. You're not actually qualified for the jobs you're applying for." It was obvious from the shocked look on her face that Crystal did not expect to hear this blunt message. A quick explanation was needed to soften the blow. "I'm not saying you don't have terrific experience and expertise. But you earned it all in the automotive industry. Any hiring manager looking at your resume will come to the same conclusion—this person could be great, but they don't know anything about health care."

Because Crystal was focusing on barriers from biases she couldn't change—being an older woman—she was missing the real challenge she had to overcome: lack of industry-specific knowledge.

By applying to the top health-care providers in her city, she was going up against literally thousands of more qualified applicants from around the world. If she was really serious about moving into a new industry, she'd have to be willing to take a few steps back on the career ladder, target smaller companies, earn less, or better yet, offer to work on some specific projects as a volunteer or consultant. She was going to have to begin to build relationships in the industry to gain credibility. Crystal had to earn her way back to the level she left behind in the automotive world. And she had to decide if she was willing to make that investment in time and money to pursue a new Buffalo.

Finding Your Tribe

When Ross was in his teen and college years he enjoyed expressing things he liked by getting colorful tattoos on his arms, legs, and neck. His tattoos showed the world who he was – a guy with many passions, a sense of humor, and a flair for design. Ross was also a finance and accounting major with serious business aspirations.

During his senior year, Ross earned an internship with a prestigious accounting firm. He gained a great deal of experience from his mentor there, a mid-career executive from a conservative background. At their first meeting, his mentor advised Ross to "keep the tattoos hidden" while in the office. Ross followed his advice and added collared shirts, ties, and two conservatively tailored jackets to his wardrobe. He did well at the firm and liked his coworkers, but did not find they had shared interests outside of accounting and work.

In the spring semester at a recruiter event, Ross met two young founders of a tech startup. They had strong coding backgrounds, an attractive business plan, and financial backing to begin building out their leadership team. Both founders were intent on creating a company culture that reflected their personalities and values—they were into rock climbing, craft beer, graphic novels, alt-music, and tattoos. They made Ross an attractive job offer after two long interviews.

The firm Ross interned for also made him an offer. Beyond the salary, this firm represented job security, a path to career advancement, and the prestige of working for a highly regarded company. The startup deal couldn't be more different—comparable salary but high risk, no name, and an extremely uncertain future. Ross's parents thought it was an easy choice to go with the established firm. But Ross chose the startup. "I felt like working for them would let me be my full self. I would have nothing to hide about who I am and what is important to me. It feels like I will find coworkers and friends there and I'm willing to take the risk to feel more accepted at work."

My point in sharing these two stories is that bias is two-sided. There are certainly people who will *absolutely not* give you the benefit of the doubt. You are not going to change them. But are you missing an opportunity by assuming it is a specific bias that makes them not choose you? Crystal was wasting her time blaming the wrong things for her difficulty in changing careers.

On the other hand, do you know your own personal biases? Before you start your search, it's crucial that you figure out what your priorities are. The work you did earlier in the program by defining your Buffalo is the foundation for your career path. Ross knew that at this starting point in his career, the culture of a company was more important to him than many other considerations.

Take a hard look at your own prejudices about the size and culture of a company, its location, and the style of work. Then do your due diligence on the company before you start applying. Keep in mind that as a job hunter I want you to always be asking the question, "Is this a company worthy of me?" If the answer is no, don't waste your time or theirs by entering the application process. Move on to better targets.

Special Challenges Are Real

As much as we like to think there's a magic formula and we may wish that everyone is going to act the "right way," that is not the case. After so many years spent placing talented people into well-suited companies, I am acutely aware that my "products" are human beings, every bit as much as my "clients" are human beings. Every contract I enter into for a talent search begins by asking the hiring manager to tell me honestly, "What kind of person do you want?" Of course, they rarely know or say everything that they hope to find. My task is to read between the lines and find the person who seems to be the best match. I make those introductions and hope they come together in ways that benefit them both. I want both parties to be happy in their professional relationship over the long term.

The world continues to change, and while I wish we could create an environment in which no one has any prejudices and everyone treats everyone else as an equal, that's not likely to ever be the standard employment situation. In your career management plan, you are going to face certain challenges that might trigger prejudice. We have to focus on how to deal with them.

Many of the people I have successfully worked with have faced bias because of their status as:

- formerly incarcerated citizens
- displaced workers
- mothers reentering the job market
- returning armed services veterans
- "necessity" entrepreneurs created by various life events like immigration, illness, or death
- older workers or "encore workers" postretirement
- workers with special needs
- young people with no real work experience

There is no one size fits all solution. Each person's situation is going to be different. But I ask every one of these people facing challenges to start by doing a realistic SWOT (strengths, weaknesses, opportunities, threats) analysis.

S—what are my special strengths?

W—where is my résumé or skill set weak?

O—what sorts of opportunities do I feel exist for me?

T—what are the hurdles that may prevent me from winning the opportunity?

The more honest and thorough you are in your personal SWOT analysis, the better able you are to set *reasonable and achievable* expectations for your next step. It's always helpful to keep in mind that the route to your Buffalo is rarely straight and fast. For most of us, the path requires "tacking," a bit of zigging and zagging around obstacles to enable us to keep moving in the direction of our goals. "Tacking" may be taking a job that seems beneath you, making a lateral move, or taking a pay cut to position you for future growth. It may be moving to a less desirable geographic location for the time being before earning a future promotion to your ideal location. It may mean investing in training or pursuing more classroom education. "Tacking" is not a setback. It's a necessary and valuable "course correction" that will ultimately move you forward.

We have all experienced the disappointment and depression that results from setting unrealistic expectations. "I'm going to lose ten pounds before the wedding." "I'm going to quit smoking this week." "I'm going to take three free online classes and be able to get a great job as a highly paid computer programmer." Change is hard. Change takes time. And it's always more likely to happen if you have someone supporting you and when you are realistic about how difficult and slow real change can be.

Getting Real to Succeed

Raymond grew up in a tough neighborhood where it was easy to fall in with the wrong crowd. He messed up, made some bad decisions, and landed in prison for several years. Being in prison gave him plenty of time to think about how he wanted to spend the rest of his life. Raymond was ready to receive some coaching advice. He was willing to spend the time and effort to do an honest appraisal of what he'd need to do to get his life back on track.

His counselor asked him to describe what he most enjoyed doing and what special skills he thought he brought to those activities. Raymond knew the answer right away. He'd been raised by his grandmother who was an amazing cook. Raymond loved to help her in the kitchen when he was young. He remembered how proud he felt when his grandmother bragged to her friends about what a good cook he was growing up to be. Making food and sharing it with people he loved, these were things Raymond enjoyed and was good at.

His counselor asked him to think about how he could make a post-incarceration career in cooking. Raymond's first thought was that he could open a homestyle restaurant. His counselor helped Raymond find some resources about the restaurant business including sample business plans, startup costs, designs, and menus. As Raymond learned more about how complicated, costly, and risky the restaurant business was, he felt very disappointed. "Don't give up," his counselor said. "If you can't own a restaurant, what other ways can you make food your focus as a way to make a living?"

That led Raymond to think more creatively about his options. He could probably get an entry-level job at a restaurant, maybe even starting as a dishwasher and then moving up as a prep cook and maybe eventually become a chef. But he also came across information about a nonprofit in his hometown that ran a cooking school for at-risk youth and operated a small café open to the public. The possibility that Raymond could share his love for cooking with kids who came from rough neighborhoods like his and use his experience to help them avoid making the same mistakes he'd made—this combination of skill and service seemed like his perfect Buffalo.

Using his time remaining in prison, Raymond took advantage of the inside training programs to advance his cooking skills. He took courses in how to become a youth counselor and began building a relationship with the executive director and staff at the nonprofit.

Having a realistic plan that he could work toward was so much better than trying to get any job that would take him after his release. Raymond still had a few years to serve out his sentence, but he felt he was *investing* in his future, not wasting precious years of his life.

When the Going Is Tough

In my business I hear the word *no* all day long. People ask me how I can stand so much rejection. I tell them, first of all, it's what I expect to hear so it's not a surprise or a disappointment. But second, I start every day with the hope (and the confidence) that after all the "no"s I am still going to get the magic of a "yes" from someone, and maybe even from more than one person. If I have been able to present a decision-maker with a candidate who has a very targeted, honest *why* document, if through the *why* document I have satisfactorily addressed all their questions and eliminated their sense of risk, at the end of the day, someone will eventually say "yes."

The first step anyone starting from a place of extra challenges must take is to get comfortable or at least accepting of the fact you are going to hear a lot of "no"s. It's not always as definite and discouraging as it sounds. It may really be someone saying, "not now" and leaving the door open to "maybe later we'll find a way to work together."

As I said before, hiring decisions are made by humans, not chatbots or AI. Yet increasingly companies are turning to algorithms to sort through online résumés as a preliminary cut. Your second task is to work hard to get past the chatbots and make contact with a human. Especially when you are a nontraditional candidate, being able to show who you are depends on getting face-to-face with a hiring manager or decision-maker. That probably won't happen if all you do is respond to online job postings.

It might help you to go back to chapter 3 and review the steps that enable you to build a network that can open doors for you. Moving your résumé from the bottom of the pile to the top will happen more readily when *a person who knows and supports you puts your name in front of someone they know is hiring.*

Once you have gotten the chance to meet face-to-face, invest heavily in preparing for the interview. Do your research about the prospective company. From their website and any news reports about them, what can you tell about what they most value? What is their company culture and work style? What image of the company do they project to the public? You'll want to take your cues from all the information you can gather and use this to avoid anything that would trigger a negative reaction during your interview.

Be sure you have reviewed any job postings on their website along with the requirements for each position. Depending on your particular background, you may save yourself and the employer valuable time by not pursuing any position you will not be able to fill. Legal barriers, advanced degrees, and certain technical or physical abilities may disqualify you. For example, some companies who provide in-home services require that all their employees be bonded. If you have a criminal record, you would not be legally able to fill a position like this. Other positions may have physical strength requirements that you may not be able to match, like the ability to lift a certain amount of pounds or operate heavy machinery. Avoid spending your time and energy on roles that are not a good match for your situation.

That doesn't mean that you have to align perfectly with every aspect of a job description. There will be situations where the requirements are somewhat flexible. Here's where the personal interview can benefit you because it gives you the chance to show you are much more than lines on a résumé. *Always remember, people hire people whom they connect with and like.*

Start by overdressing for the role. Your first impression is powerful. You want to send a clear signal that you are professional, mature, motivated, and someone to be taken seriously for the value you offer. Remember that hiring decisions always carry risk for the company. Your job in this interview is to convince the manager that you will be hardest working, most reliable employee who is determined to do your job better than everybody else. Tell your story with an emphasis on your *why* document; in what *specific ways* will your experience result in adding value to the company?

As you are defining who your target companies are, look at smaller or younger companies first. Often it is going to be much easier to get your foot in the door and be able to speak with a real person, even if initially it is just over the phone. Be prepared to make an offer that is hard for them to refuse. Whether you are a woman returning to the workforce, a veteran looking for civilian employment, or a young person with no real job experience, offering to volunteer your services to demonstrate your value can get you a shot at regular employment.

Starting from Zero

Melanie's husband took a job in Sydney, Australia, and while it was a terrific opportunity for him, it meant Melanie had to give up her law practice in the United States to relocate. Finding work in a country in which she had no contacts, no professional reputation, and no knowledge of the legal system was a high hurdle.

Melanie started researching legal firms in the Sydney area and reached out to five small to midsize firms with the same offer. "I'd like to work for your firm and with my experience, I know I'd be a great addition to your team. To show you what I can do for your practice, I'm willing to volunteer my services for thirty days. If you don't see the value after a month, don't hire me. No obligation at all." Three of the five firms immediately said yes. They liked her confidence and her willingness to put herself out there at no risk to them. Waiving a salary for thirty days resulted in landing a great job with a firm that proved to be a perfect fit for Melanie.

The tactic of volunteering instead of asking for a full-time position may also be effective for "free agents." If you've lost your position for any number of reasons—downsizing, company acquisition, company closure, et cetera—why not consider offering to show what you can do for a company you'd like to work for? I was working with a man who was between roles and didn't have a ton of previous experience. He asked the hiring manager at one of his target companies to let him come in for a few weeks to observe and help out in one department. The man came to work for four weeks without getting paid. He bonded well with the work team and was able to show his work ethic along with his willingness to learn. After a month, he was brought on full-time. In that first year he made more money than he ever had in his life. An "unpaid month" proved to be one of the best investments he could have made. I call it a "working interview."

A variation of this approach can be effective for older workers who may be looking for an "encore career." For people who either don't need or want full-time employment with a long career horizon, offering to take on short-term projects as a consultant or be hired in an "interim" role can provide a valuable solution for both an employer and for the employee. Employers are often reluctant to fill a full-time position with someone without prospects for a long career horizon. They are reluctant to invest in someone who may only want to work for a few more years. Limiting the company commitment to be project specific or to a particular time frame represents much less risk and a more definite ROI for the employer.

Now I understand that everyone can't afford to work for a month for free or take work on a freelance or project basis. What can you do to reduce the level of uncertainty and risk your unconventional background poses for a manager? How can you show that you're the one who should get the job? How can you prove that what you claim about your skills and attitude are true?

Sometimes it requires taking a few steps back, accepting a position you are overqualified for, and earning your way up the career ladder by consistent, reliable, hard work. It's as if these lower-level positions are a kind of "working interview" that will convince the company to open more opportunities for you because you've earned them. You should never accept a position you will resent having to do, however, because having a sour attitude will ensure it will end badly. I always tell my clients they should never go into a job with the expectation that they are going to be leaving it by a certain time. By the same token, don't take a job for the sake of being employed. If you are not truly engaged with and rewarded in some way by the work, you are unlikely to thrive there.

You've set your Buffalo and you know chances are you're going to do some tacking along the way. It may not be your ideal job, but if it keeps you on the path to your dream goal, seize the opportunity even if it is less than what you hoped for now. View it as a way to earn income as you continue to work on your plan to get to your Buffalo.

Seeing Leads to Believing

Andre had time in prison to think hard about what he wanted for himself and his loved ones when he had a chance to change direction. Following the WYB program, he was able to identify a small company that showed it was willing to hire formerly incarcerated workers. Andre prepared for his interview by learning as much as he could about the company and by writing his *why* document thoroughly. But the hardest part was practicing what he would say about himself.

When the interviewer asked Andre to describe what he brought to the company, Andre was ready. "I don't think there is anything that will prevent me from being an outstanding employee. While I was incarcerated for eight years, I made a decision to turn my life around. I completed my associate degree and I have nearly completed my bachelor's degree. I am determined to work as hard as I need to convince you I'm honest, dependable, and highly motivated. I am ready to work harder than anyone else and take on the jobs no one else is willing to do. I have made some serious mistakes, and now I am trying to rebuild my life. Earning a living at a good job is an important piece of my success. I'm asking for the chance to prove that I mean what I say."

Andre's honesty and positive attitude swayed the interviewer, who gave him an opportunity. Within six months, Andre was promoted to a supervisory role. He had proved that what he had done in the past should not be used against him to limit his future potential.

Going Your Own Way

One bias we haven't mentioned is about independence. Some people really will only be happy being their own boss. That form of freedom can take many different shapes. You might:

- start and operate your own business as an entrepreneur
- be a "fractional worker" on a part-time basis with a number of employers
- work in the "gig economy" for companies like Uber or Door Dash
- explore potential franchise systems that could align with your goals.

Increasingly being "your own boss" appears very attractive for many people of all ages and backgrounds. But it is definitely not for everyone.

If you have already been in the workforce for some time and are thinking about changing careers, before you jump, take a critical look at the things that you're doing. Is it where you work and who you work for that makes you unhappy? Or is it about the type of work you do? Do you need to change companies or change careers? Changing companies is obviously much easier, but it's not worth doing if what you really crave is being able to do a different type of work altogether.

Perhaps you have reached mid- and upper-level management roles and believe you are not part of the succession plan for senior management. You've hit a ceiling but feel there is more you could and would like to accomplish as an entrepreneur.

Or you are fresh out of college, have tons of energy, a lot of confidence and a "great idea" for a business. Frankly, it's always easier to pursue an entrepreneurial venture when you have nothing to lose. Later on, the adult responsibilities of a mortgage, family care, education expense, and retirement savings add to the amount of risk and can outweigh your desire for independence. While I never discourage young people from pursuing an entrepreneurial urge, I am frank about how stressful and hard it is to launch and run a successful business.

If no job, no matter how much it pays, where it is, or what the work itself involves will get you to your Buffalo, then going your own way is worth pursuing. Soon you won't be alone. Current projections for the future of work in the United States indicate that a variety of economic and demographic factors will push about 50 percent of the population into entrepreneurship, freelance work, or fractional contract jobs. Opportunities are changing fast. More than ever, it is up to you to decide what your work life will look like.

Ready to Set Sail

Throughout this book, I have been encouraging you to answer the big, all-important question: Where's Your Buffalo? Through this program I've provided a proven road map to help you figure out your unique answer. Now I'll let you in on a trade secret. There's a group of people we in the talent search trade refer to as "Can't Help Candidates." These are the people who may listen and nod when we offer advice. They might even say they are going to follow it. But at the end of the day, they do nothing but complain about how unfair it is that no one will hire them for their dream job. Don't let yourself fall into this category of underachievers. Take charge and take responsibility. You can do it.

Follow all the steps the WYB program teaches. Setting a plan is where it starts. Work hard on your *why* document, be thoughtful and realistic about targeting potential companies and positions, and be prepared to explain your situation. Be honest about your strengths and skills gaps. Take ownership of any mistakes you've made or time you've spent out of the workforce. But make it clear with specific examples that, if given an opportunity, you will show how valuable an employee you are.

What's most important as you complete and implement the WYB program is for you to be able to evaluate each opportunity and feel confident to decide if it meets *your criteria*. You are a talented job hunter, keenly aware of the value that you bring to an employer. I want you to continually ask, "Does this position get me closer to my Buffalo?" When you've done the work to create choices for yourself, you can say, "No, I don't want this one. I'm going to take the better offer, the one that keeps me sailing to Buffalo." I look forward to seeing you arrive.

CONCLUSION

Insights from an Executive Search Consultant

During my many years as a talent search executive, I have helped thousands of people reach their Buffalo. Over that time, the work world has certainly undergone many changes. But I believe one thing is as true today as it was decades ago: everybody has the *right* to find and do and get paid for *work that they enjoy*.

Don't get me wrong. I'm not claiming that every day on your WYB job is going to be paradise. Every move in your career is not going to be a straight shot upward. There will be hard times, or as the sailor in me likes to think of them, choppy waves and gusty headwinds that might slow you down, push you off course, and require you to alter your route a bit.

Reaching your Buffalo doesn't guarantee you've found nirvana. This is a hard journey and even at the end of it, you may find you've reached most but not all of your goals. But isn't having 80–90 percent of your dream far, far better than being stuck in the rut of unrewarding work and pointless job searches? You bet it is.

In chapter 7, I revisited the idea that the foundation of the WYB process is about you answering the big, all-important question: Where's Your Buffalo? No one can answer this for you. So, start there and then keep in mind the other important destinations along the WYB road map.

- **Remember the "big rocks."** These are the things that matter the most to you. The things that give meaning and even joy to your everyday life. Get the "big rocks" in place before you start obsessing about the small pebbles. Fill your imaginary "job jar" with all the elements you hope for in your most fulfilling vision for your life. If you get the "big rocks" handled, you'll find the small ones fall into place more easily as you sketch out your plan. Your short list might include deciding which of the following are big or small rocks:
  - What you enjoy doing—what activities come with the job?
  - Location—how much does where you live and work matter?
  - Compensation—what is your lifestyle? What are your financial goals?
- **Be realistic** about what you can do using the skills, training, background, and education you bring to the job market. Be honest about your willingness and ability to fill any gaps your ideal career requires. Are you financially, physically, and mentally able to pursue more training or education? Can you afford to do an unpaid internship or volunteer your time to acquire some on the job training and expand your network? Have you done your due diligence to learn what the people in this line of work actually do every day? Can you genuinely imagine yourself enjoying working in this environment?
- **Embrace** the idea of pursuing positions you are legitimately qualified for and at which you'll be successful. If you ignore the basic requirements employers expect from candidates, you are probably setting yourself up for constant disappointment. The hiring process for managers comes down to minimizing risk. They don't want or need to "take chances" on a candidate. Be confident you can present

yourself honestly as fully qualified for the role. This does not mean you have nothing to learn in the role. Surely you can have some "stretch" goals. By all means, don't limit yourself to only go after jobs that are below your level of experience. But be honest about what value your experience brings to the employer.

- **Put some pins in a map.** Remember it's not just the type of work but *where that job is located* that should inform your search. If you are unable or unwilling to relocate, don't waste your time and the hiring manager's time pretending to be a viable candidate. Before you begin your target list of potential employers, narrow the field to companies within your acceptable geography.

- **Let honesty guide you.** We've all made missteps, bad decisions, and outright mistakes. Be candid about yours, especially if these have kept you out of the workforce. Your past does not have to limit your future. Take ownership of your history but be very clear about how your past experience has brought you to a place and time when you are ready, willing, and very able to make a valuable contribution to the employer who hires you. Go beyond empty claims like "I'm a people person" to provide specific examples of how your experience translates into skills that will benefit the employer.

- **Prepare to compete.** If there's a job out there that you want, chances are many others, sometimes even *thousands* of others, also want that position. Only one person will get the job. Use all the WYB steps to give you a competitive advantage. Do your homework, have your *why* document customized for the employer, make a professional appearance, and practice all the techniques for *closing* the offer. Recent studies have shown that people who negotiate for a higher salary at the time of hire have been increasingly successful. Even though success is far from guaranteed, you can be sure you won't get an increase if you don't ask.

- **Build your network in two directions.** Eighty percent of all jobs are filled through internal hires and networking before these jobs are ever posted on the Internet. Going back to the hiring process being focused on minimizing risk, hiring managers prefer to fill positions at all levels with people they personally know or someone who comes recommended by someone the manager already knows and trusts. Chances are you have been helped by someone in the network you've built. Keep nurturing and expanding that network since these are the people who will most likely continue to help you move *up*.

  Once you've had some success and are in a position to help others, build your network *down* by extending your help to those trying to get established or move ahead in their early careers. Mentor, volunteer, make introductions, or speak at school events. Just don't be that person who doesn't return a phone call unless there's something in it for them. Be willing to devote some time to face-to-face meetings with people seeking your advice or help. Take some time to listen and help when and however you can. Sooner or later, and I believe it's sooner, you will be glad you did.

- **Stay calm.** Decisions driven by panic or desperation rarely work out. There are going to be unexpected developments that rock your plan. Companies get acquired, layoffs happen, economies tank, jobs are outsourced or redefined. It's stressful and painful.

  But you have an advantage because you have a process to follow. There will be lots of people giving you advice, most of it not useful. Be proactive. Take control of your next move. Revisit your Buffalo and apply the methodology you've been practicing.

  Even if everything remains stable in your current company, our situations change over our lifetimes. Family changes, goals and aspirations evolve, values and needs shift. Over time your Buffalo will most likely need to be revised. The WYB methodology becomes part of your life forever.

Looking back on my career, I've had about eight different Buffalos. The world changed and so did I, but the process has remained reliably effective. Using new technologies has only made it even more powerful. Each time I needed to plot a new course to a new destination, I already knew how to proceed as a job *hunter*, not as a panicked seeker asking anyone and everyone to "please hire me."

I Thought I Was Unemployable

At a recent networking event I ran into Kim, a sixty-one-year-old woman I hadn't seen in over a year. When I asked how she was doing, she replied with a huge smile. "Never better." Of course, I wanted to hear more so she filled me in on her recent job search.

Kim had spent decades in the restaurant business in a variety of roles. While she loved the company she worked for, she found herself exhausted by the relentless stress of her job. She did not feel that she would be physically and emotionally capable of continuing to work under these conditions until she could afford to retire. She had been trying for a couple of years to find a way out of the restaurant industry. She told me she spent years applying for literally hundreds of jobs online. She never even got one response or one interview. She had begun to believe that as an older woman she was "unemployable." It was depressing to be constantly rejected. She thought she was fated to keep toiling away at her super-stressful job until she could retire in a few more years.

Meanwhile, one of her neighbors was recovering from an illness. Kim kindly made her neighbor some chicken soup. When Kim brought it to her neighbor's house, the neighbor's husband answered the door. "I was just thinking about you," he said. "We have a job opening where I work that I think you'd be great for."

Long story short, he was able to get Kim an interview for a project manager position in a highly technical firm. Kim was hardly a shoo-in for the role. She was not a certified project manager. However, she drew on her many successes in the fast-moving restaurant environment to demonstrate her skill at fostering employee engagement, hitting deadlines, and successfully implementing many new programs and initiatives for her current employer. By thoughtfully evaluating her skill set and accomplishments, she was able to point to her extensive restaurant management experience to prove she was "the sort of person who always gets things done by encouraging people to do their best."

Kim had to be patient. Conversations with the potential employer went on for nearly a year before they made her an offer to become project manager for their workers' compensation portfolio. When I saw her at the networking event, Kim had been in the new job for six months. "I am happy to say this is by far the best job I have ever had. Instead of counting the days to retirement, I am looking forward to many more great years working for this company," she said.

That explained her big smile.

I'm sharing Kim's story because it confirms so much of the advice this book contains. Even though Kim had never heard of the WYB approach, she was applying some of the key elements of the Where's Your Buffalo? process.

- People and relationships matter.
- Your network is hugely valuable.
- Skills are transferable.
- Responding to online job boards is wasted effort.
- Formal credentials do not have to be a barrier.

- Age does not have to disqualify you.
- Patience is required.
- The *why* document and openness to people and new possibilities are keys to advancing your goals.

I wrote this book to help people just like Kim. People who think there are too many obstacles preventing them from finding meaningful, satisfying work. People who don't have a clear way to evaluate what they are currently doing against what they want. Proactive job hunters who need a way to make a plan and evaluate choices and decisions according to their plan.

Where's Your Buffalo? is a process that empowers you to follow a proven approach to identifying, pursuing, and getting what you hope for. It's a lifelong journey. Along the way we all make mistakes. But when you are clear on your Buffalo, utilizing the WYB process is like using Google Maps for your career. Input your destination wherever your Buffalo is to be found and follow the route that unfolds.

I am here to coach you and encourage you to achieve huge success on your journey. Connect with me on LinkedIn and find more programming and resources online at MyHuntPath.com. Consider me part of your network. Starting today, begin your plan for a brighter, happier, more productive and satisfying work life, and it can be yours.

Afterword

I want to thank you for buying my book and allowing me to help you find your Buffalo. But this is just the beginning. This is a process, and I will be there to help you on your journey. Let me offer you a couple of other opportunities and suggestions.

The first thing I would suggest is to connect with me on LinkedIn. Please follow me. I am going to be offering podcasts, webinars, and posts that will relate to your career. I have also created a LinkedIn group called "The 130% Club," which I invite you to join as well. The concept of the group is that I hope everyone will achieve their "Buffalo." Along the journey, I want to help you leverage the services of a recruiter; they will help you find a new and exciting role and they will earn a fee for introducing you to an opportunity. This means that a company or organization has paid a 30 percent premium for the opportunity to hire you.

For those of you that are committed to building a career plan, I can also offer you access to my career management platform. MyHuntPath (www.myhuntpath.com) offers a complete career management course that includes thirty-three videos and related worksheets. If you email or text me a picture of you holding my book, include your email and I will send you the code that will get you a 50 percent discount on the course.

My goal is to let everyone in the world know what "Where Is Your Buffalo?" means, so feel free to share this information with anyone that you think needs help building and managing their career.

I am also aggressively working on building strategic partnerships with high schools, colleges and universities, alumni organizations, and staffing and recruiting firms that want to leverage my material to help people build a plan and become better prepared candidates. If you are interested in exploring partnerships, speaking engagements or seminars, please reach out; I am always glad to help.

Many times over the years I have had people go through my program—which is basically teaching everyone how to be a headhunter for themselves—approach me on exploring the possibility of recruiting or searching as a career option. If this is something you're interested in, please reach out and I will try to help. In my opinion, a career in recruiting is awesome. I spend my time helping companies grow, introducing life-changing career opportunities to candidates, and helping people manage their careers. This is my Buffalo, and I would be glad to help you explore that option.

My contact details are:

Thomas K. Johnston

Tj@synovasearch.com

Cell—216-789-9850

Finally, I did not want this book to just be my voice. I believe everyone can gain insights from anyone willing to sit down, have a cup of coffee, share their story, and offer their advice on their career management.

With that in mind, I'd also like to offer you the perspective and expertise of other high performers. The following pages are a collection of interviews I conducted with colleagues from a variety of backgrounds regarding career management. This highly accomplished group of people have achieved incredible success in their chosen careers and include CEOs to college students. My plan is to do full interviews with them in my upcoming podcasts, so keep your eyes open for announcements.

I did not want to make this too complicated, so I asked each for some general thoughts around careers and then to give advice to early job seekers, those in the middle of their careers journey, and finally, advice to those that are seeking to move to the executive suite. As you may have noticed throughout this book, I also hold a special place for Returning Citizens, so I have also included a good friend, Brandon Chrostowski, to address the special group of people.

Appendix 1: Career Management Advice from the Experts

Howard L. Lewis
Founder, Family Heritage Life Insurance Company

From humble beginnings in the poverty-stricken streets of Covington, Kentucky, to the pinnacle of what many would describe as the American dream, my journey has been one of resilience, learning, and understanding the power of people. I give sincere thanks to the mentors, friends, colleagues, and institutions like the Boy Scouts of America, the University of Kentucky, and Xavier University, which undeniably helped shape me into the kind of person who would go on to build and eventually sell a business with over $1 billion in assets. I pen the following advice with the utmost conviction that it can help you to chart your own prosperous and fulfilling career path.

What advice would you give someone just starting their career journey?

Explore, then Commit: At the beginning, dive into various fields to better understand your interests and strengths. When you find a field that suits you, narrow your focus and invest your energy thoughtfully.

Stay Curious: Never stop learning. This can be through formal education, reading, mentors, online courses, seminars, or hands-on experience.

Cultivate a Network: People are your greatest resource. Connect with professionals in and around your desired field. Networking can lead to mentorship, advice, and job opportunities.

Be Open-Minded: The early stages of your career oftentimes require you to be flexible in terms of roles, responsibilities, and even locations.

What advice do you have for individuals in the middle of their career?

Evaluate and Reflect: Objectively and subjectively assess your career path thus far. What have you enjoyed, what have you excelled at, what have you learned, and where are you headed?

Sharpen Your Sword: Advances in modern technology have ignited a breakneck pace of change in every industry. Stay relevant by continuously updating your skills.

Seek Mentorship: Mentors provide invaluable advice, networking opportunities, encouragement, accountability, perspective, wisdom, confidence building, and role modeling.

Build Leadership Skills: Even if you're not in a leadership role, developing these skills can be critical for advancing your career.

What are your suggestions for experienced candidates trying to move to the executive suite?

Serve To Lead: A real leader is a servant in CEO's clothing. Prioritize the growth and well-being of your people. Lead with empathy, foster a culture of participation, and demonstrate values like courage, integrity, and humility. Your success as a leader is shaped by how high you lift others.

Strategic Networking: Early in your career you networked with a shotgun approach, but now you need to use precision. Connect with individuals who are in or aligned with the executive suite.

Sell *You:* Develop and promote your own personal brand. This does not mean simply wearing a black turtleneck every day. Spotlight your unique experiences, skills, and vision for leadership.

Executive Education: Consider that Executive MBA or certificate program you keep receiving emails about. It's time to set yourself apart from the pack with new skills and insights specifically designed for executive leadership.

What is do you think is most important for returning citizens who are seeking employment?

Embrace Your Story: Life is a journey of redemption no matter how far you've risen or fallen. Be honest about your past but focus on your commitment to the future.

Seek Help: There are many organizations and programs specifically designed to assist returning citizens. Utilize these resources and you will find support, patience, and understanding.

Crawl, Walk, Run: Your first jobs will not be ideal, but you should see them as stepping stones to regain confidence in yourself and build a recent work history for future job applications.

Continuous Learning and Development: Demonstrate your commitment to self-improvement by actively engaging in educational opportunities. This could involve enrolling in vocational training, attending workshops, participating in online courses, or acquiring certifications.

In closing, to each of you, at whichever stage of your career you stand, remember this—your career is a saga that unfolds with every decision, challenge, and triumph. Embrace each moment of this journey, for it is uniquely yours. May your paths be illuminated with wisdom, courage, and an unyielding desire to be effective, not only in your life but in the lives of others.

Peter Quigley
President and CEO of Kelly Services

I am a lifelong believer in the dignity of work and an enthusiastic advocate for flexible, nontraditional, and modern ways of working. As the proud president and CEO of Kelly, my goal is to connect vital talent with great organizations, helping everyone thrive. I'm always ready for what's next, and for me, that means helping break down societal barriers that prevent all people from accessing enriching, life-changing work opportunities.

What advice would you give someone just starting their career journey?

I think the most important thing is to have a plan and that starts with evaluating what you want in your professional career. The plan will change, no doubt about that. But to have a plan that you can come back to and revisit as your career changes is a really important thing, because it'll force you to explore what you want out of your career, and ultimately what you want out of your life. I would recommend that they have a plan for their life as well. But starting with a plan for their career is a good start. It can change, it is very dynamic, but if you don't start with a plan, you're really just winging it and hoping for the best.

What advice do you have for individuals in the middle of their career?

Well, I think that at that point in the career it's important to take stock or take inventory of where you've been. Look back and focus on the things that you have been good at, the things that you have enjoyed, and the things that you know, to which you bring a different level of engagement. Inventory them again; create some kind of reflection on the past ten years or whatever the period is. Try to calibrate what the next step is for the individual and use it to stress test what you're looking at in the future.

What are your suggestions for experienced candidates trying to move to the executive suite?

I would encourage people to get out of their comfort zone. As I reflect on my own career, the times when I have taken what could be considered a lateral move or special project are the times when I chose to get out of my comfort zone. I think that's ultimately what prepares you to be a successful executive. You can just climb the ladder and you could potentially get there, but I think being willing to take some assignments that may not be in your wheelhouse yet is a great way to gain new skills and demonstrate that you have a field of vision that is broad enough to handle what a C-level position requires: breadth, vision, capability, and energy.

Brandon Chrostowski

Founder, President, and CEO of EDWINS Leadership & Restaurant Institute

Brandon Edwin Chrostowski is an award-winning trailblazer in the reentry and incarceration space known for impacting culinary and hospitality training both in and out of the nation's prisons while preserving French cooking traditions.

His mission-driven effort to train and hire former prison inmates at his flagship French restaurant and nonprofit has created a national model for reentry and an educational pipeline for the formerly incarcerated to learn the discipline and skill of fine dining.

With a less than 1 percent recidivism rate, his impactful social program provides more than one hundred formerly incarcerated adults with free culinary and hospitality arts training each year. Since founding EDWINS in 2007, Chrostowski has reinforced his mission by creating the EDWINS Second Chance Life Skills Center, a campus that includes housing for students, family, and alumni, a library, fitness center, kids' park, and garden as well as providing other wraparound services for his students. The latest addition to campus is the EDWINS Family Center, which provides free daycare to EDWINS students during class and service. EDWINS offers a virtual curriculum to more than 400,000 inmates at prisons across the country and on-site programs at Grafton Correctional Institute and Cuyahoga County Juvenile Detention Center.

Chrostowski's culinary footprint has also expanded with the opening of Edwins Too, a restaurant and culinary incubator, EDWINS Butcher Shop, and EDWINS Bakery and Diner. All establishments offer deliciously affordable dining opportunities to the Cleveland community and provide careers for EDWINS graduates who want to remain under the EDWINS umbrella.

A classically trained chef and sommelier, Chrostowski honed his skills at fine dining establishments in Paris, New York, and Chicago, including Lucas Carton, Chanterelle, Picholine, Le Cirque, and Charlie Trotter's.

Recognition of his culinary efforts include 2023 James Beard Finalist, IFMA's 2020 Silver Plate, CNN 2016 Heroes, Crain's "40 under

40" Awards and the Richard C. Cornuelle Award from the Manhattan Institute for Social Entrepreneurship. Chrostowski was also the subject of the 2018 Academy Award nominated documentary *Knife Skills*—a short film following the opening of EDWINS.

Published in national outlets and sought after to speak at recognizable platforms, Chrostowski has a Bachelor of Business and Restaurant Management and an associate degree in culinary arts from the Culinary Institute of America.

What advice would you give someone just starting their career journey?

You train you and your team to serve others and everything great will follow.

What advice do you have for individuals in the middle of their career?

When I talk to people that are a bit more mature in their career and looking to make a change, I'd say the same thing. You must— mentally, physically, spiritually—train harder than an Olympic athlete so that you can finish last to serve others, and everything else will follow. It doesn't matter what age, what career, or what stage; if you're not training, you're not trying. You will never succeed in what you're trying to do if you don't focus on others. You might succeed with money. You might succeed with real estate. You might achieve things that many will consider success; but you won't succeed, you won't be fulfilled. If you want to be great, you can't put yourself first; you have to train and take care of yourself and prepare yourself to be the best, but in order to serve others—that's the trick and that's the secret.

What are your suggestions for experienced candidates trying to move to the executive suite?

A big part of my career has focused on helping returning citizens to rebuild their lives. Everyone deserves an opportunity to pursue a fulfilling career. When you have some prior history—a felony conviction—challenges are bigger. The road is a bit rougher, but you can still be successful. The advice I would share with a more senior person is pretty much the same, with an extra bit of seasoning: it's going to take time, you're in for a long road, but again, if you continue to try to be your best in order to serve others, the world cannot help but to get behind you. If they see someone continue to give and work their hardest to help others succeed, you're going to be at the top of every management team.

Another option is to take the ownership route. If people want to work with and for you, people will want to work and follow you. I think it's a really, really big issue that we can handle better. If you're coming out of prison or if you just got put into prison, it doesn't matter. You just continue to train your best, your ability to give it to others. But again, that caveat is it's going to take time. It may take five or ten years, it's not going to happen overnight, but that consistent road is a life well lived.

At a point in your career, you may decide to become an entrepreneur or run. My advice is to spend someone else's money first before you spend your own. Work yourself up to a management level or quasi ownership level. You get to see the mistakes that cost money. Do it on someone else's dime. There's going to be a point where you have to take that leap. You must take the leap and ride the bull and a lot of people don't have the courage that it takes to make that move. It means putting your ambitions, your personal estates, your family in a risky spot and but those who make the jump, they know what it is. Then it's contagious. You want to take another jump, another jump. This idea of entrepreneurship becomes addictive, but you must make the leap. If something were to happen, I wouldn't feel bad at all if I tried my best to help others. You're going to need wings so when you take that jump, you're going to fly.

Robin Toft
Global Life Sciences & Boardroom Diversity Leader | ZRG Partners

Robin Toft is an inspirational leader, board director, and the award-winning author of *WE CAN: The Executive Woman's Guide to Career Advancement*. Robin is committed to elevating women worldwide by educating companies on the competitive advantage of building inclusive leadership teams. *WE CAN* was recognized as one of the top 100 Best CEO Books of All Time by Book Authority and provides the confidence, language, tools, and practical advice for women to design and realize the career of their dreams. Both *WE CAN* and her second book, *Ignite Your Board Career: Board IQ Playbook*, are available on Amazon.

Robin is renowned for building high-performing organizations by recruiting women and underrepresented candidates into top roles and overcoming unconscious bias in hiring. She has served as Global Life Sciences & Boardroom Diversity Leader of the fastest-growing global executive search firm ZRG Partners. Prior to joining ZRG Partners, Robin was founder and CEO of Toft Group, an executive search firm focused on the placement of female executives in life sciences and health-care high-tech. Her company rapidly grew to over $10 million in revenue before Toft Group was successfully acquired by ZRG Partners in 2019. Prior to founding Toft Group, Robin served twenty years as a biotech executive. Robin currently serves on the multiple board of director roles for companies advancing women worldwide.

What advice would you give someone just starting their career journey?

- *Listen to your internal voice*: I believe we are all here for a very specific purpose—your act of service to the planet—like an acorn is programmed to be an oak tree. Obviously, certain careers have more accolades, et cetera, but you are wise to choose your passion since it is the path to great happiness and wholeness in the end.

- *Choose your path carefully*: I advise keeping "Do what you love, and the money will follow" as a central mantra at the core of your being. In the beginning, try to choose a practical path to what you love, where you can make money, but as a path to *what you love*. It may sound crazy, but in truth there is no substitute *for doing what you love, with whom you love*—it is the path to prosperity. For instance, while in college I wanted to become a high school science teacher, but fortunately was guided by a wise guidance counselor to work in a medical lab, since there would be immediate income upon graduation. Later, about ten years in, I pursued my teaching credential, but then sales were more lucrative.

- *Build confidence*: Just have faith and *confidence* that you will be happy and successful if you continue to work hard in that direction. So, for now, know that you are collecting experiences along that path, and never, ever give up. There are, however, many ways to get to your destination, so be open-minded and *flexible* as to how it will happen for you.

What advice do you have for individuals in the middle of their career?

From ten to twenty years, you will be building *competence* in the areas for which you will become recognized. At this point, you have been collecting experiences for ten years. If you are still living out another person's dream for you (your parents, partners, et cetera), realize that and shift into the ideal path for you personally. If you look hard at your career to date, you will find that there is a golden thread that runs through your career life, and you should be able to pick it up now from within the fabric of your life's work to date. Once you reach your golden thread, it will continue to be the thread and consistently make you happy, regardless of the career you choose.

Be humble and grateful: Ask for feedback from peers, direct reports, and bosses. Gratefully accept it, internalize it and create personal goals each year. Track your achievements.

Create value, ask for opportunity: While working in the lab about five years into my career, I raised my hand and became a leader (teacher) within a lab setting. About ten years in, I gathered the courage to ask to be in sales. I had to leave the company to do it, but I was the top performer my first year at the company I joined! Turns out with this approach of educating my clients, doctors, nurses, et cetera, I quickly began being recognized as a sales star, and then I earned the right to ask for even more opportunity within the companies I served, and leverage what I have learned.

Lastly, *build connections*. Internal and external. The people you work with, particularly in a large global company, will make or break your career success as you take on greater roles and responsibilities.

What are your suggestions for experienced candidates trying to move to the executive suite?

At this stage of your career, I believe it's all about the people, leadership, and the team; however you must be working within the right culture so choose carefully.

Be sure you're able to bring your passion to work and make a difference in the workplace. Wake up every day and determine how you can add most value to the organization you serve. Your job is to make your CEO or other leader and the company you serve even more successful. Demand that you personally—and all your team are—signed up for the mission, vision, and values of the organization; and live and breathe them. If they are not aligned with the mission and/or don't have the right capabilities, then make changes *fast*.

If you have a team, focus on leadership; tell them you are building the best team they have ever served on—the one you personally want to work on. Create annual goals and your team's goals with the company as a whole and deliver. I believe employees need "I trust you, I believe in you, I empower you" leadership these days. Since there is a lot of skepticism, you need to earn it one by one. Get in the trenches with them in order to win their hearts and minds. Ask them to be honest with you when things are going well and demonstrate this value as you lead them. Lead with purpose, integrity, honesty, and transparency, and you will be happy regardless of the challenges the company needs to face. Teamwork truly does make the dream work and will create the success you desire. I've learned the secret of success is giving and receiving as much love as you can in your lifetime—do it at work and at home.

Abid Hamid
Non-Executive Director—Acumen International

Experienced CEO in fast growing businesses and startups. Abid has been the Group Chief Executive officer for a PE and VC specialist firm for the last 6.5 years. He is building the preeminent VC house for the staffing industry, which started with the UK and seven investments and today it has twenty countries and over thirty-five investments in the portfolio. He is experienced in running culturally diverse teams, operating in challenging environments, addressing business issues, facilitating turnarounds, and building and growing companies. Abid has traveled extensively in Africa, the Middle East, Europe, Asia, Australia, and the United States.

What advice would you give someone just starting their career journey?

Most people "fall" into a profession or a job without giving it much thought. They are influenced by the choices that they made while studying, and were pressured by their parents and suggestions from friends. A few aspire to follow people that they admire. Because this decision will be the most important decision that you will ever make, there is little or no professional help when entering the market. We certainly don't teach careers at schools and universities. We may have career advisors but beyond that there is little insight into career choices and real life advice at entry level. Fast-forward fifteen years and we have been in the same field since we left education and whether we regret our decision fifteen years ago or not, most individuals either don't get the opportunity to change that decision or are not lucky enough for events to point them in any other direction in their careers. A few, a lucky few, make the right choice the first time and the rest is history.

What advice do you have for individuals in the middle of their career?

I have interviewed well over five hundred thousand people in my career as a recruiter and as a CEO and director of various businesses.

I have made big blunders in my choices but happily more good choices that have led to working with some talented and great individuals. What makes them great and why were they good choices?

Let's start with the individual.

In the last five years I was asked to help advise senior military officers who were transitioning from the military to the commercial world. These are men and women who have achieved much in their careers, are leaders, have seen adversity and are robust people. They are the elite of the military; they lead troops in battle, overcome their enemy; they lost colleagues and their charges in this role. One would have thought these are people who do not lack confidence, who don't hesitate to make decisions and are comfortable in leadership. However, one of the most interesting parts of this exercise was how these supreme leaders of men and women of action were completely at a loss on what they would be good at in the commercial world. They are losing a real and clear goal that they have lived with for the last ten to twenty years—cocooned in a world that has a defined moral code and duty, focus that is unwavering—and going into a world that doesn't meet these exacting standards. Their security blanket of the military family, traditions, camaraderie, and structure are no longer going to be there.

What greeted me were very experienced people who were almost devoid of confidence in what they would do next and whether they would be any good at it.

What are your suggestions for experienced candidates trying to move to the executive suite?

My first advice to them was the same for any senior person: You are lucky! You have a second chance to build and define your career—so let's start with these questions below. To answer these questions, you must be honest, clear, and without prejudice about any career. Don't define a job title.

What are your nonnegotiables? This is an interesting question as most people don't know them. List them. They become the core of what is not flexible, such as "I do not want to join a particular industry" or "I want to work within a team, not on my own."

Make a list of things that you like doing. Like . . . really like doing it.

Make a list of all the things that you are good at and whether you like them or not.

What is the financial aspiration? It doesn't have to be shot for the stars.

What are you no good at or don't want in a job?

This exercise needs then to be evaluated. Someone must challenge every one of your answers. As these are challenged clarity starts to form—a wheel where your nonnegotiables sit in the middle and everything else works out from there.

The purpose of the exercise is to define what you genuinely want and then add reality to it. ("I want to be working in anti-poaching in Africa, but I need to earn $120k per year.") This starts to narrow down the choices that are available to you in the real world.

Now that we have extracted the above, we need to start to fit it into an actual job. If you don't start with the ideal role for you when you are making these decisions, what will happen is, you will take the first decent role that's offered to you, and you are back to where we began. The aim is to get as many of the things on your list in a role that you will apply for.

Gary Buckland
CEO Lexitas Legal Services

Gary Buckland is currently the CEO of Lexitas. Gary joined Lexitas in March 2015 as the chief operations officer of the company and was promoted to CEO in June of 2017. Gary also serves on the board of directors for Lexitas, IMS Expert Services, which is the largest expert witness search firm in the United States, as well as Juris Medicus, a medical case review company. Prior to joining Lexitas, Gary was the vice president and business unit leader of Kelly Legal Managed Services, the former legal staffing solutions business unit of Kelly Services, Inc., from 2007 until 2015. Prior to joining Kelly in 2007, he served as CEO and president of the Atlantic Group, a part of the public human capital and consulting company SearchPath International, where his company specialized in permanent placement of attorneys and litigation support to the legal industry. Gary also served as President of Legalink Corporation, a global court reporting, legal videography, trial presentation, and litigation support company, prior to their acquisition by Merrill Corp. Before joining LegaLink, he was vice president and general manager with Olsten Staffing, where he was responsible for fifty-seven branch locations throughout the United States. Additionally, he spent fourteen years with Motorola Inc. in various management positions in sales, operations, and marketing. Gary holds a bachelor of science degree in business management from Old Dominion University in Norfolk, Virginia. He is a member of the American Management Association.

What advice would you give someone just starting their career journey?

Networking is critical. Leverage your connections through family, friends, school, church, et cetera to learn about opportunities and get introductions.

Don't be afraid to ask for informational interviews or advice from your network. People are often willing to help, especially if there is a close connection.

Developing your network early will pay dividends throughout your career as you progress and take on new roles.

What advice do you have for individuals in the middle of their career?

Take time to identify your passions, interests, and goals. What type of role or industry excites you?

Be open to lateral moves or switching industries/companies to gain new skills and experiences. This will make you a more well-rounded candidate over the long term.

The job market is hot right now. Use this to your advantage to make a desired career shift if needed.

What are your suggestions for experienced candidates trying to move to the executive suite?

For those who have more than fifteen years of experience in senior management roles in either operations or sales, your experience is of value more than you may know. I was one of those who aspired to work for larger organizations in senior leadership roles and was fortunate enough to be an asset and contributor. However, as satisfying as working in those Fortune 500 companies was, I found that I was not being utilized to my full potential. I then was introduced to the private equity industry, and my career really took off. Many PE firms are always looking for senior leaders to become C-suite members of their portfolio companies. The need for professional management is paramount to drive scale and growth and organizational development within many of these companies. It is an opportunity to use your experience while building wealth through performance. Opportunities abound, so take a broader look at growth-oriented PE portfolios. Gaining experience at a large corporation can provide important credibility and learning. At the same time, taking an entrepreneurial role at a smaller company can help develop critical skills like strategic planning. Blending these big companies and entrepreneurial experiences can best position you for executive roles. Be selective about advanced education like an MBA. Make sure it clearly aligns with your goals.

Getting to the C suite may require stepping back strategically at times to obtain the right mixture of experiences.

The key is having clear goals and a plan to build the right skills. Be open to lateral moves and even taking a step back at times rather than a straight path upward. With the right mix of experiences and timing, you can position yourself for that executive office.

Elizabeth Johnston
Rowing Student-Athlete at Michigan State University | ImpriMed
Marketing & Customer Support Assistant

I am a rising senior and student-athlete at Michigan State University. I am a captain on the Michigan State women's rowing team, where I coxed our Varsity 8+ at the Big10 Championship the past two years. I am currently studying for a bachelor of science in animal science with a focus in pre–veterinary medicine. My passion for this field started from a very young age with my involvement in riding horses and showing dogs. I knew I wanted to help animals in any way that I could. I have been able to shadow various veterinary clinics throughout the years, as well as complete an internship with a veterinary biotech company in the summer of 2022, and work part-time during the school year. I hope to obtain more knowledge and experience in the field of veterinary medicine and pharmaceutical sales. I am interested in changing my career path, looking into sales and marketing roles.

What advice would you give someone just starting their career journey?

I think, especially from a young age, it's important to get experience wherever that is because a lot of high school and college students just do basic jobs. I think it is important to find what you're interested in and try to shadow or do an internship. I would recommend that high school and college students just network and talk to people. I attended a presentation that focused not on who you know but who knows you. I think that's really impactful, because so many of us are told the opposite.

I think that we need to leverage the people we know, classmates, teachers, friends, parents, and parents of friends. People need to take advantage of those resources when they are available, because once we are out in the working world, some of those opportunities are not available. I tell people to reach out to alumni, build your network, talk to people. Having people know who you are and know what your interests are is a good way to start on a career path.

My story is simple; from a young age, I've always been interested in veterinary medicine and being a vet. In high school I had an opportunity to shadow a vet. I learned how a vet office runs and operates. I had this passion, and it grew, this is why I decided to get my undergraduate degree in animal science with a pre-veterinary focus, with a plan to go to vet school.

However, in my junior summer I was able to secure an internship at a company called Imprimed. They started in 2017, commercialized in 2021. Their product takes blood samples from canines and uses artificial intelligence to give the best chemotherapy treatment for thirteen different cancers in canines. The first internship was in the lab, then I had a second internship in marketing and sales, which kind of was very different from what I thought my original career path than going to vet school. This allowed me the opportunity to work with their commercial operations team on marketing and sales. I realized that I really like the flexibility that it gave me, and that it provided an opportunity to collaborate with people in the animal health field.

So, I decided to change my focus to animal health sales and marketing.

One of the most important things is networking. I think a lot of times I talk to people, and they lament that they do not have a network. What they don't realize is that their family, their friends, the parents of their friends, all have connections. I know so many people that don't really have a very full résumé, they don't have a lot of previous jobs and opportunities. Networking can be scary, but unless you do it, you're not going to get any better at it. People like to talk about themselves and give advice. You've got to be proactive.

I had the opportunity to spend some time with my VP of sales at a national trade show. It was pretty interesting. I think sales are something that most people are quite afraid of because you're going in not knowing anybody and trying to sell something, but he really spends most of the time asking people what he can do to help them. And as a sales rep, I think that's the most important thing you can do: find ways to help them and make their life easier. Most people are afraid of sales; they hear the word, and the first thing they picture is somebody trying to sell you something. You don't want to be a used car salesman, but great salespeople solve problems. They represent products and services that solve problems.

Megan Durham
Owner and Managing Partner, SearchPath of Columbus

Megan has over eighteen years running a successful recruiting practice focused on the pet industry. She has been married for eighteen years, is a mother of three, and is passionate about rescuing animals.

What advice would you give someone just starting their career journey?

When you are trying to decide what you want to do with your life, it is important to remember that most often it is not a straight line. Rather, it is a long and winding path to get to your career. You should have the mindset that it is unlikely you will find the perfect career right away. I think a lot of kids today struggle with that. The first thing you must do is talk to people; you must get out there and you must use your network. I have heard a lot of young people say they don't have a network. You do have a network—it is your friends, family, the parents of your friends. You should include professors that you're working with because I am sure they have a lot of connections in different industries. Talk and build relationships with the people you meet at internships and different activities you're doing through college. You have a lot of different people in your network that you should be talking to and learning about what they do and what their jobs are like, especially things that are related to what you're getting a degree in. Have a curious mindset and try to learn more about what other people are doing.

Eventually, you will talk to someone that you think has a job that sounds intriguing and interesting. You must learn about it. There are so many different things out there that you can be involved in and not just focus on the top things most people think about when looking for a career, like being a doctor, lawyer, veterinarian, teacher, or fireman. These are the basic jobs, but there are thousands and thousands of other things that you've never even heard of, and you won't hear of unless you are talking to people and trying to learn about other things.

The next suggestion is that once you do start to explore what you're interested in or sounds intriguing, you need to find a way to do it and not just talk about it. You need to try doing it at an entry level to be able to learn what the role really entails. Most jobs are not exactly what you think they are, and every job has cool parts and not-so-cool parts. Whatever career you are leaning toward, you need to make sure that you can handle the not-so-cool parts as well. The only way to learn that is to explore the job with an internship or job shadow.

What advice do you have for individuals in the middle of their career?

You're still going to have to use your network and reach out to people and talk and actively work on taking that next step in your career. The difference here is that you should have a lot more of a network to pull from at this point. People who are professionals that you've worked with and gotten to know over the last ten to twelve years. This is a situation where you want to be more tactical versus just casting a wide net like you might do earlier on in your career. I think it's important to reach out but be very selective about the people in your network that you reach out to. Do your research beforehand.

Reach out to people that you trust and share some details about what you've done and outline some of your accomplishments. Share some details about your company and the products that you have worked with. Ask to set up a conversation to see if there's any opportunity currently or down the road and try to have high-level career conversations with people at companies that you are striving to be a part of or with people who are in roles that you are aiming for.

What are your suggestions for experienced candidates trying to move to the executive suite?

For someone looking to get to the executive suite, the most important thing is being able to prove, based on your career history, what you can bring to the table. In most companies, there are only a few people in these kinds of roles, and I think that to stand out from others, you really need to have the accomplishments to back it up. If you look at what you're bringing to the table and it doesn't compare, you're probably not in a position to take that step yet. I think your focus should be on driving numbers and driving revenue in your current role so that when you put together a list of your accomplishments, they speak for themselves.

Bob Weiler
Managing Partner—Brimstone

As the managing funder of Brimstone Consulting Group, Bob Weiler works with business leaders across a range of industries to improve the growth and profitability of their organizations, drive large-scale change, and develop leaders. As an advisor to CEOs and C-suite executives, Bob has been instrumental in helping leaders achieve alignment, identify and develop next-generation talent and CEO succession candidates, and energize the organization. Bob has consulted with Fortune 500 Global firms and Fortune 100 firm, while also assisting large non-profit and government organizations. Prior to launching Brimstone, Bob served as president and CEO of Grand Circle Travel, a global enterprise—comprised of a family of travel companies committed to changing people's lives by offering high-impact experiences to travelers and building local communities through philanthropy, social entrepreneurship, and volunteerism. Bob also served as the associate director of the Global Leadership Program, a renowned executive development program at the Ross School of Business at the University of Michigan, and taught executive education courses in leadership and leadership development courses at the University of Michigan's Ross School of Business. Bob worked with leadership expert Noel Tichy at General Electric's Crotonville Training Center to design key modules for developing high-performing teams and individuals. And as executive vice president of the Hurricane Island Outward Bound School, the largest of the Outward Bound schools in the world, Bob helped build the school's professional development program. Bob has captured his decades of experience advising and accelerating some of the world's leading organizations in his book, *The Core Four: Harness the Four Core Business Drivers to Accelerate Your Organization*. Bob holds both BA and MA degrees from the University of Vermont. He is a licensed US Coast Guard captain and private pilot. He believes that one should strive to push for their maximum human potential. Bob regularly competes in ultra endurance events: Ride Across the Sky in

Leadville, Colorado, the Spartan 50-mile Peak to Peak, and the 2021 Sea to Summit. He resides in Camden, Maine, with his wife Wendy.

What advice would you give someone just starting their career journey?

My first book is called *It's About You,* and I think that's the first thing that I would say to a young person if they're expecting this to just magically happen without you putting in hard work. Some of the key questions are around location, your interests, what makes you happy, what kind of work do you like. Do you like to collaborate with people, or do you prefer to work by yourself?

You know all these questions are important when you're putting together a plan. You need to take a deeper dive and understand what you might be willing to give up getting the job you really, really love. That's following your passion. Location isn't that important. I think your whole focus comes down to what you're passionate about. If you have a job that you do not like, you spend eight to ten hours a day being miserable. If you're passionate about your job, it is not going to feel like work at all. You're going to get up every day, and you're going to get up before dawn and go to bed after dark because what you're doing is what you love to be doing. And I think those kinds of questions that are outlined in the book are exactly the right questions.

I few years ago I had a very good friend's daughter call me about a role she was considering. She graduated from a top university with an MBA in sustainability. The issue was that the role was in Hershey, Pennsylvania, and she was not sure she wanted to go to Hershey. I told her to take the job, the location is not that important because the role with a huge company was exactly what she wanted. She took the job, and she has had an incredible experience. She loves her job, and her experience will allow her many options down the road.

What advice do you have for individuals in the middle of their career?

This is when you have someone that has done well where they are but they are starting to think about what is next. They want to stay with their current company or make a change and move to another company. In our coaching, we discuss a concept called "the perfect calendar." We sit down and ask them to put together a perfect calendar. The goal is to lock down on what they like to do and how they like to spend their days. Everyone has a different vision of what a perfect day would look like; what if you could live this day seven days a week? You would not care who you work for because this is exactly how you would love to spend your days. If you don't know what that looks like, you need to figure it out. How can you have a great week if you don't even know what a perfect calendar looks like? If your calendar is driving you and you're not in control, you need to make a change. You need to find out what you're passionate about and what do you want to do.

What are the things you don't like that you'd like to do less of? Can you get that opportunity in your current company? Do we need to look outside to another company? Do you need to make a pivot to a different role? You know, this is usually the time people start thinking about doing something a little more entrepreneurial.

What are your suggestions for experienced candidates trying to move to the executive suite?

What does that next opportunity look like? What should they be looking forward to doing? We spent a lot of time around that space and that's a pretty tricky question. Are you happy in the industry you know? If the answer is, yes, I love the industry, I love where I am, I love the work I'm doing but you are not seeing the growth opportunity because your company just hired a new CEO, you need to look outside. So now the real deep question again: we give you a white piece of paper to outline what you like to do, and we sit down do some pretty serious reflection here for yourself, because you got to say: I love this industry. I want to stay in this industry. And I don't have any options here. So, what are my options? What? What really can I do? We spend a fair amount of time as you do in your book, trying to get them really, really clear about options. Do we burn the boats? Are you ready to leave?

Of course, we recommend, as is outlined in the book, to go to your network first. Start talking to some people out there. At this point you must figure out how many people you know in your industry.

At this point in your career, it is a different game. So now go right back to those questions you have around location, income. Are you willing to take the job as a CEO if the location is not ideal?

The key to your career: take the call, help people, because someday you might need their help. Spend a little bit of time, have a cup of coffee occasionally to give people some direction because they're going to be the ones that are going to help you when you need it.

Allan Hartley
Founder and Managing Partner, Nextwave Growth Partner

Allan Hartley has fostered growth and profitability in every enterprise he has led throughout his career. He started his career at Robert Half, where he managed and became one of the highest producers which led him to start the contracting division for KForce, which subsequently went public. As the founder and former CEO of Accountabilities, Hire Technologies, and Staffing 360 Solutions, all of which successfully entered the public markets under his guidance, he has navigated the complexities of scaling businesses, overseeing mergers, and facilitating acquisitions. His approach is always firsthand and strategy-driven, focusing on creating robust action plans, streamlining operations, and spearheading initiatives that directly contribute to revenue growth and market expansion.

What advice would you give someone just starting their career journey?

I would start with: be eager, be excited. You want to go into the process with enthusiasm. For any job you have at the very beginning of your career you must show eagerness and enthusiasm. You must show that you want the role. You've got to want to learn and understand the process, follow the process. I was fortunate in my career because I started with Robert Half, and it was all process oriented, very activity driven. I decided not to focus on the money; I focused on the process, I did the activity. I realized that if I did them well, then the money will follow.

I never thought about the money. I knew that if I did my job and did it well, I'll make my money—because I know the way that they paid, and it was based on performance. So, I say to everyone: be eager, follow the process. I went over what I was supposed to do and remembered, it's an art not a science. Whatever they told everyone to do, I did more.

What advice do you have for individuals in the middle of their career?

Increase your visibility. You need to make sure that people see what you are and what you're doing. If you do what I said in the very beginning—increase your production, increase your activities and all that—that activity gets revenues. If you increase your visibility, they'll see that. When you get into the middle management cycle, that is where you learn my trade. I worked hard to exceed in my trade, I got visibility, I got noticed, and sure enough, eventually I'm running the office.

People started noticing me and our competitors started noticing me, that helped launch my career. Raise your hand, volunteer for the hard projects, go beyond your job and take initiative. Take leadership roles when offered. When I was offered a leadership role, I didn't even hesitate, and I exceeded in the role. You must be able to collaborate with the people; you are only as good as the people that are on your team.

You're the quarterback of your team. A good quarterback makes their players even better. If you're a leader, you need to make sure your people are doing well because your performance is also based on how well your team does. Regardless of what you do, you always can advance into leadership, mentorship, and management roles. Take those leadership opportunities. And in today's world of social media, it's pretty easy to get your story out there and build your network and let people know when you're accomplishing great things.

What are your suggestions for experienced candidates trying to move to the executive suite?

Be innovative, that is where you start. You need to have great communication skills. I ended up being a CEO of some publicly traded companies, and that was a big deal. I had to go on road shows and sell the story. Being a leader, you must show passion. You must be passionate about what you do. I'm very passionate. I talk with authority and passion; I think that's a big deal. I keep going back to it. Go beyond what's expected. If you do the things to be innovated, build your communication skills. Be a leader. Be an innovator. One of the biggest keys, because it sets you apart: you must be a differentiator. Set yourself apart from the herd, then you'll definitely move up.

Dennis Kozlowski
Chairman of the Fortune Society—Investor/Former CEO

L. Dennis Kozlowski grew up in New Jersey and received his bachelor of science in business administration from Seton Hall University in 1968. Upon graduation Kozlowski held various management positions at SCM Corporation in New York City and Cabot Corporation in Boston, Massachusetts.

Kozlowski joined Tyco International in 1975. At that time, Tyco was a small ($20 million revenue) technology-driven company. He and his team commercialized the core technologies of Tyco. In 1989, Kozlowski was appointed chief operating officer of Tyco International, in 1990, he was appointed CEO, and he was named chairman of the board in 1991.

Under Kozlowski's leadership, Tyco grew into a global giant with over $40 billion in revenue and a market capitalization of more than $110 billion. The company employed 260,000 people in sixty countries. Much of the growth was accomplished by high-profile worldwide acquisitions. Under Kozlowski's leadership, Tyco constantly ranked as one of the fifty largest and most profitable companies in the world with its growing medical, security, electronic, flow control, and telecom businesses. Dennis parted ways with Tyco in 2002 in a controversy that is well documented in Professor Catherine Neal's book *Taking Down the Lion*.

Dennis Kozlowski received a Doctor of Business Administration from the University of New Hampshire, Honoris Causa, and Roger Williams University. He currently resides in South Florida and New York City with his wife, Kimberly. He has M&A and business consulting practice. He also served as chairman of the Fortune Society of NYC, where he supported efforts to help for formerly incarcerated individuals gain meaningful careers, housing, and ongoing counseling to help them to reestablish themselves into their communities.

What advice would you give someone just starting their career journey?

Try to pursue something that you have an interest in or passion for.
I think is overused because it's hard to know you have a passion for

something until you get into it. But if you have a knack for business or an interest in business my advice would be: make sure you have a background where you understand how to read a business financial statement. You don't have to be an accountant, but you need to know how to keep your score. So having the ability to keep score yourself without having to have somebody else tell you how you're doing, that is a big advantage in business. I attribute some of the success I had in business to the fact that I could read the P&L and a balance sheet.

I could not tell you the rules of accounting or accepted accounting principles work, but I knew enough to know how I was doing. When I see people coming out and into the business world now and they're in general management positions, or even presidents of divisions or operations, and every month they have to go to the finance guy and say, how am I doing? The finance guy is now controlling the president or the CEO or the general manager or whatever is heading up the business.

What advice do you have for individuals in the middle of their career?

This is where life changes for you. You've gone from being promoted now to being elected and being elected is a different process than being promoted. You know you've got to deal with your constituents, and that includes the board, maybe the CEO.

You've got to be able to deal with people on a lateral basis in the various departments you're working with, and you've got to be able to deal with and motivate the people that are reporting to you. You know you've got to show the ability to work at all levels of an organization. You've got to take the time to be known to the people that are going to elect you.

When the CEO says, I want to promote this guy to a CFO, CTO, or chief marketing officer, whatever the title is—the person is making the decision to promote you. You are known to that group of people that are going to elect you.

Not having people knowing you, mentoring you, or supporting you in that job is a significant reason why people don't succeed at it. Once you get that job, once you're there in order to achieve success in that job, be certain to replace yourself. Far too often, people will go up to that job and they have a comfort factor from the last job that got them that promotion and they're trying to do two jobs and they tend to gravitate toward the last one they did, and they never really become the CEO. They stay stuck in the mud with their old job. Get somebody good to replace you assuming you know you've been savvy enough to get elected to the job.

What are your suggestions for experienced candidates trying to move to the executive suite?

I think it's important somehow, some way, along the line, to gain the wherewithal to have some confidence in looking at a business financial statement and know what it says. It's not that hard. It just takes a little time to learn how to understand where the revenue comes from and how expenses are paid. If you're doing well and on track and on plan, I think that's awesome. You do need to understand the basics.

There is a reason why they've been promoted a few times. They've been promoted because they did a good job in their last job, as they're looking to move further up in the organization and take on more responsibilities. Take a fresh look at everything that you're being held or going to be held responsible for; don't accept things the way they are and don't believe the old cliché, if it's not broken, don't fix it. Look at everything that is going on and follow your curiosity. Be curious about how information comes together and how conclusions are made and you'll find lots of time when you dig into the decision-making process. More decisions were made based upon information that may not have been totally accurate but were the opinions of people; you could go down the road of opinions as opposed to fact.

I've seen that happen far too many times. So, stay curious. Be very curious about everything you're responsible for and look behind the scenes for that support.

William Kubicek
Principal at PCRecruiter

William, an entrepreneur, and creator of PCRecruiter, the leading Recruiting and Applicant Tracking Solution, has been in the technology field since his early career. His company is growing steadily, both domestically and internationally. Dealing with Hong Kong, Japan, China, all of Europe, Australia, along with both North and South America, William's knowledge of international trade became extensive.

PCRecruiter Applicant Tracking Software (ATS), Software as a Service (SaaS), Recruiting CRM, Recruiting Software, Full Outlook Integration, ATS Implementation

What advice would you give someone just starting their career journey?

My career has been a little different than most. I don't necessarily see myself as a Fortune 500 type of guy. My advice is that you should always keep your ears open and actually listen to people that have been successful. Listen to what they have to say, and then try to ask them questions to dig in on what they're saying to you, so that you can gain knowledge. When you're younger, connect with someone with a little more wisdom and experience that you can leverage as you go through your career. It's especially critical. It's always important to be listening. What does the customer need? Listen to your employees and learn from them. This is especially important early in your career.

I started out in sales. A lot of young people don't like sales; they move away from them. They've got bad impressions of it, but it wound up being the basis of where I started building my career. I got that first role through networking. I went skiing with my dad, and we were at the bar. I was talking to different people letting them know I needed a job. It was in 1992. There's a recession and I have a degree in environmental engineering. I did very well at school, but nobody was hiring engineers. Someone said, "I don't want to talk to you about a job now but come to my office at 7:30 a.m. on Monday and we will talk then." I got there at 7:30 in the morning, and it's a winter day and the parking lot is completely empty. There's nobody to be found at any of the businesses in the office building. So, I just sat in my car, and I knew what kind of car the guy drove, and I sat there until about eleven in the morning waiting and the guy showed up, and I got the job. They paid me $12,000 a year plus commission. It worked out well, I got a bit of equity, and it launched my career in technology and sales.

What advice do you have for individuals in the middle of their career?

It's a competition. You've got to be in your game all the time and you got to be willing to take risks and jump ahead. You've got to do a little soul-searching and you've got to say to yourself, "what do I like about this job, what do I not like about this job?" That's a little tougher than it may seem because most of us are out there and we're following the dollar. If you only follow the dollar, that's tough and, you're not going to be happy and you're not going to excel in your role if you're not happy.

Look at what you like or don't like and then look at the business and see if there is an opening, or if you can create an opening to do what you want to do. I would suggest you go to your senior management team and tell them what you want to do and how it will benefit the company. Most executives focus on benefits that create revenue or will make people's lives easier. Put together a solid pitch. Why do you want to do that within your organization? If there is nowhere to grow in your current company, then the next thing to start is to looking outside your organization. Build a network outside your organization with those people that are doing what you want to do.

What are your suggestions for experienced candidates trying to move to the executive suite?

If you've gotten to that level where you're ready to step into the C suite, you probably understand the importance of continuous learning. What you talk about is how to build a team. When you're talking with your CEO, you want to talk about building your team, whether that's in HR or in any other thing you want to talk about in positive lights. The team members that you've helped succeed in their wins are more than your own because as you get to the C suite, it's not about what you do it is what the people you hire do for you.

You want to also be talking about how you delegate things and examples of the things your team has accomplished. If you haven't done those things, you're probably not ready for that conversation. You should drop those things down and do those things if you're not doing them.

Go to LinkedIn, join groups, and participate and get involved in the community. As much as I don't love the LI beast, you have got to be active and build your network. It is critical and if you don't do it, you're not going to be found by recruiters; in general, you want to be found easily. Be sure to be ready to be found, even if you're not looking to be found.

Help people when they reach out to you and be very targeted. It does no good to have fifty thousand connections; you need to get a manageable number. A couple of hundred people that are in your industry is about right. When they reach out to you, help them, so that when you reach out to them, they'll help you.

Kennon Kincaid
CEO, Odgers Berndtson US

Kennon Kincaid is the CEO of Odgers Berndtson US, a leading executive search and leadership development firm. Odgers Berndtson's clients come from every shape and size of organization: from startups to multinational corporations, and span the private, not-for-profit, and public sectors.

Kennon was promoted to the role of CEO after four years as the Odgers Berndtson US Chief Operating Officer, where he oversaw its people, processes, and operations. He serves on the firm's Board of Directors as well as its Global Advisory Board.

Prior to joining Odgers, Kennon served as a diplomat, advancing the interests of the United States and its allies across Europe, Africa, and Asia Pacific. Subsequently, Kennon joined Rocket Lab, a leading aerospace company and launch service provider, where he established and led international business development, security operations, and government relations.

Kennon serves on the Board of Directors of the U.S. Civilian Corps, a not-for-profit that is part of a broader movement to reinvigorate and enable a culture of service in the United States. He is an active member of Alder, a community of executives working to foster generational leadership, and is a Board Member of the Miners Wrestling Club. Kennon speaks French and has a bachelor of international studies (with honors) from Virginia Military Institute. He is a proud husband and father of three.

What advice would you give someone just starting their career journey?

> I love to say to people, young and old, does your career story make sense? Looking backward, right? It usually does not. I think we want it to be this perfect linear, straight line. We graduate college and we're looking forward, but I think what we find is as we move through each decade, where we may end up is not necessarily where we would have thought we'd be when we look back at, say, age forty or fifty or sixty.

If we've done enough of the right things, I think we'll look back and our career story will actually tell a story and be quite linear in retrospect. I look at my own journey. Who would have thought that I would go from the military to some unique government service, then to a space Launch Company and end up as the CEO of the up-and-coming executive search firms?

No one could have choreographed that story at twenty-three years old. I know I wouldn't have come up with it if I tried. We all know that search is a fantastic career and I think smart people who are passionate about the world of work could become recruiters at some intersection in their life, but I think the theme of my own story—which I think is also the theme of so many—is that you allow yourself to be open to opportunities and you allow yourself to understand the core of your skill set. I think if you understand the core of that, you can take it into so many different industries and markets. Then you're following people and purpose through your career. That's what I think is the advice I give to absolutely everyone: understand what it is you're good at, which could be what you studied or not. Maybe the guidance your parents or teachers have told you align, but it is important to allow for adjustments as you move forward. You want to work with great people, strong leaders, and to have some purpose that inspires you in life. I think that we naturally take on the kind of path of journey to success. For some there might be more ambition to that than others and there's nothing wrong with ambition. I think people use that as a negative. I think ambition means different things to different people. Sometimes you have to back up to go forward. This is where you really need to understand who you are first and foremost. Understand how you tick and then seek out individuals that you respect or want to be around, and then you overlay a little bit of purpose to that. Your career path tends to make sense. Everything I just described has a degree of authenticity, both internal and external, intrinsic and extrinsic. I think it's not talked about enough. I think we spend a lot of time thinking about what's on our CVs or résumés and what those things look like. I actually think the entire contour of our careers are about relationships. You need to know how to develop those skills and stay true to them. I always tell young folks: know who you are. Be open-minded. Surround yourself with great people and the rest will sort itself out.

That may sound too easy, but is quite difficult because I think the world is full of so much noise. We must constantly think about what that noise is. I go back to that core blackboard which is to know yourself and be intentional. We surround ourselves with people to share our journey.

I think those little principles can guide you to life success. There's got to be a lot of good old-fashioned hard work layered in there. We want everything to be easy. Nothing's easy. And, I think easy, and work, is a relative term as well.

What advice do you have for individuals in the middle of their career?

I think it goes back to relationships. I think it's got to be a theme that your really nurture throughout your life. I think we have, particularly in this day and age. There's the opportunity to have so many connections and contacts. I look at LinkedIn and I joke: I'm kind of a big deal on LinkedIn. I've got thousands of relationships. I look on Facebook and I've got hundreds, if not thousands of relationships. What it really boils down to is: who are the ten or fifteen people—maybe not even that many that you take the time, during your professional career, and there may be some overlap in personal that you've really invested in. I think what I found and many other very successful people have found, is it's within those relationships that we identify our next opportunities.

It's a group of people that you know will always answer the phone and will always be in your band. Suddenly, you have these concentric circles of relationships.

I'd say I have fifteen of these kinds of relationships, key and close professional contacts. They also have their fifteen, and that list goes on and on. I think you can find jobs on LinkedIn and working with great recruiters, it is within that network of networks that you're going to find that next great thing. It may be that they come and pull you or maybe that you arrive at this juncture on your own. You should always be asking, what's next for me?

I truly believe that is where you're going to learn. That's an authentic investment in time and relationships. I'd also encourage you to have a recruiter or two in that mix because they're a good group to include in your network.

What are your suggestions for experienced candidates trying to move to the executive suite?

The first question you need to ask is why I am the right person for the top job. I recommend that people bring new ideas, show them what you can do. Become something more than what you're currently doing, be proactive. You must be willing to take on projects that nobody else wants. Show them you can get things done.

I think it's there's only a handful of people that can elevate. If you're a director or VP in a Fortune 500 company, that next jump might be a mid-cap or private equity back business. Sometimes it is better to go smaller than bigger. Try to find that team where you feel as though you can jump in and lead it to the next level. I often hear from my private equity associates that the first CEO-ship shouldn't be your last one. It's your opportunity to really set the stage as to what you can do. Never be afraid to jump into something that may feel smaller than what you set out to do. If you use that as a catalyst to drive great purpose and success into the next role. I also think many of us suffer from imposter syndrome. I would contend that most great CEOs suffer from imposter syndrome. They have the title. They live in the world every day, but they don't think they deserve it. I think it's a healthy sense of humility that we all need to bear. I always encourage folks to reach for higher opportunities but also think about what they believe and what they can attain. For so many, I think they're actually setting the bar too low. On one hand, I tell folks to think about the right size and fit for you where you're going to be welcome and be able to come and lead.

Is your skill set as a VP going to be enough to make that next jump? The other question is about setting the bar too low. I think many of us feel as though we don't deserve something, or we haven't earned our chance to be a CEO. Let someone else be the judge of that. Put yourself out there, don't be afraid to ask for the challenge. Don't be afraid to raise the idea that you may be ready for that next step in your career.

Surround ourselves with A players; even if you don't think you're an A player yourself, surround yourself with A players. I heard a great recruiter just the other day say A players hire A players; B players hire C players. We are the sum of the circles we surround ourselves in, so surround yourself with the very, very best people when you're heading out on a mission and careers. No different, no different than that.

Kevin Anderson
CEO and editor-in-chief, Kevin Anderson and Associates

Kevin is an accomplished ghostwriter, #1 national-bestselling author, editor, and entrepreneur with a wealth of industry knowledge and professional experience. He has worked with numerous bestselling and award-winning authors, prominent literary agents, Big-5 publishers, and a long list of public figures, successful professionals, and aspiring authors. He is also a contributing author by invitation to Publishers Weekly's *Book Publishing Almanac 2022: A Master Class in the Art of Bringing Books to Readers* and the author of the #2 *Wall Street Journal*, #1 Barnes & Noble, and #1 Amazon bestseller, *PhDone: A Professional Dissertation Editor's Guide to Writing Your Doctoral Thesis and Earning Your PhD.*

Both a creative writer and a scholar, Kevin earned his master's degree at Harvard University with a concentration in literary theory and criticism. While at Harvard, he studied under poet laureate and critical theorist Professor Michael D. Jackson and honed the literary criticism skills upon which he built his career in the book-writing and editing business.

As CEO and editor in chief, Kevin oversees all operations at his firm. He enjoys working closely with clients and makes himself readily available by phone and email throughout the planning, ghostwriting, editing, and publishing process. He is an invaluable resource and dedicates his time and expertise generously to ensuring his firm's clients receive the best-quality service in the industry.

When he's not collaborating with authors, agents, and publishers, you may find him reading Nabokov, Cormac McCarthy, or Proust; surfing the northeastern shores; composing music; fishing for striped bass; debating philosophy; brewing Belgian-style beer; wakeboarding with his family and neighbors; or enjoying the arts, culture, and food of a faraway place. Of all life's pleasures, Kevin most enjoys the adventures he shares with his wife and their four children.

What advice would you give someone just starting their career journey?

I would say to be open to opportunities and not afraid to jump on them. You know I didn't come from a business background at all, but I saw opportunities, took risks, jumped on them. I also was not afraid to abandon them if they started to look like they weren't working out. It is all about looking for and finding opportunities and being open to them. This approach has let me to six different businesses, several of which became eight-figure businesses in annual revenue and that's all from someone that had no business background.

When I look back, it's all been a series of recognizing opportunities: feeling the need and just making it happen.

What advice do you have for individuals in the middle of their career?

It might sound like it's too early. but start thinking about your exit plan. And I don't mean necessarily start thinking about getting out. I mean that you should start building the structures around you and under you that allow your business or whatever you're doing to sustain itself without you having to be critically involved in every detail.

This can mean different things for different people, and it depends on the business. No matter what you're doing, no matter what business it is, even if something that really depends only on you, if you're the main asset—you can still build structures and people and have things around you that propel your business. Build a board and a team that can handle all the things that drag you down and keep you from doing what you're best at and what you love most. I know that sounds like a lot of different ideas, but it's kind of the same thing. It is about untangling you from the stuff that you're not the best at and making you and your ideas into a company versus just making it about you. You can become a more self-sustaining asset and build the team around you to support you.

What are your suggestions for experienced candidates trying to move to the executive suite?

I would tell them that if they're in a place where they have found joy and they feel a strong connection, to really look at what causes that—and to take that with them, because those are the values that they have within what they're already doing. And if it's something that they are passionate about, to be able to translate that and to maintain that within the organization is crucial.

And how are you going to live? How are we going to embody that? What are the ways that we're already doing what we love and what do we need to change? How do we continue to move forward? How is it that we do that in such a way that we don't have to tell people they see it, or they feel it?

I think it is very important to not forget what it was like in the level that you are currently in, as you're looking ahead, because you wouldn't commit to further time in a space if you didn't love what you were doing, or you didn't feel passionate about it.

Someone who's successful on that C-suite level is someone who can maintain that level of connection. You should not forget where you came from and understand the position they're in, and how their perspectives may be a little bit different.

As you look to make the step up, are you prepared? Do you have the people to lead after you leave? The best leaders are the ones that do that well and consistently.

Treva Offutt
Visual and Performing Artist, Actress and Teacher
Treva has had the honor of working with many dynamic dance/theater/ music ensembles including NYC's Urban Bush Women, Belgium's Remote-Control Productions, Ireland's Daghdha Dance Company, and India's Adishakti Theater Company. She most recently appeared at Dobama Theatre in *THIS* (Marrell). Recent productions include *Rasheeda Speaking and Passing Strange* with Karamu, *Love Loss* and *What I Wore* with Mamai, *Cole Porter* on Broadway, with the Cleveland Jazz Orchestra and The Musical Theater Project as well as special joint production between Karamu and TMTP The Impact of Shuffle Along. Treva is a member of SAG/AFTRA and in her tenth year directing at Heights Youth Theater and teaching Performing Arts at Laurel School.

What advice would you give someone just starting their career journey?

The advice that I would give them is that your major is not your career. You should keep an open mind to all possibilities. My trajectory has been very unusual, but I followed my passions and have found a career that has encompassed all those passions.

Part of what that meant was doing things and learning what I do like and what I don't like by experiencing different types of careers. In the beginning of my career, I was touring. I was performing all over the world. I've always been touring between visual and performing arts. I ended up going to Rhode Island School of Design, where I majored in illustration and minored in animation. A week after college I started training in set and lighting and choreography. I went to Brown University and took courses in medical illustrations. One of the things that is a requirement is that you know animation, which is how I ended up minoring in animation. I took medical courses. I did animation. I also toured for about twelve years straight. I left the road, and I worked as an arts administrator, as a director of education and outreach at the Kitchen in New York City. I was able to build on my passion for teaching as well. My mother is an award-winning educator, so I grew up surrounded by education, and it's been at the forefront of my heart. Since I was little, I was with the Urban Bush Women, which was my first company. I did a lot of training about community engagement and community outreach. I really like working with people where they are and growing from there. I really encompass all those things in the way that I approach teaching.

So, all my experiences have come together. I never thought I would be teaching full-time as an in-class teacher. I did that for twelve years and I really enjoyed teaching. The benefit of taking everything in when I was on the road was learning from different places and different people with different approaches. The training that I received with the Urban Bush Women I worked with and the People's Institute for Survival and beyond helped me with my teaching career.

So, it all kind of comes full circle as you just follow your journey. Look at new opportunities and don't be closed off based on what you think your major was in school.

What advice do you have for individuals in the middle of their career?

Well, one of the things that my father taught me is you always make pro and con lists, which was one of the things his generation did. That is different from my generation. They stayed in the same job for their whole lives.

Sometimes we become complacent, and we're not living what we're passionate about. Sometimes people have fallen into something that was safe or was great financially but is draining them emotionally or is not feeding their spirit.

I tell my daughter to leverage the benefit of keyword searches. You can do all kinds of things and look them up so quickly. We need to do personal keyword searches for ourselves.

What is it that I am passionate about? What is it that I would like to do? What is it that I want to dedicate the next ten years to doing? You need to take stock of that and see where I am right now. We need to ask if it is in alignment.

I heard a speaker at Laurel when I was teaching there; she is a science evangelist. She spread the word of science, and she said something that was beautiful to me. She said "If your head, heart, and gut are not in alignment, it's not the right choice." She also said that redwood and bonsai are from the same seed. It's just about the environment. To that point, I think it's very important to continue to do a self-check. There may be aspects of what I do that I love, but if I could go further, or if I could do something different. What would it be?

Are we following a path because someone said, have something to fall back on, be safe?

I think a lot of times when we're young, that's what you know. It's all about getting out of school, getting a job, starting to gain possessions and building a foundation. But then, suddenly, you wake up one day and say, okay, I'm doing something I'm really not that excited about. I'm interviewing a candidate right now for a role where he's literally going to take two steps back in his career to get back to the part of the he actually liked. He's been elevated and promoted, but he said, "I don't like being up here. I like more hands-on down here," and he said, "I'm willing to make that sacrifice."

What are your suggestions for experienced candidates trying to move to the executive suite?

> Be innovative, show the people around you what you like and what you need from them. You can get lost by just being a hard worker and getting lost in doing what you know and what you like doing. If you're boring and not noticeable, you're not going to get noticed. You might do your job really well, but you need to think about ways to prove value to the existing C suite. Show that you have ideas. Show that you are capable of thinking outside the box. Take initiative to do things that help the company and that you are more than your exact job description. You don't have to go off the rails and do something without permission, but bring in those opportunities to the C suite that show that you're a forward thinker. The C suite needs people that can solve problems, so show that you're that problem-solver.
>
> Navigate where you want to go.

Appendix 2: Examples of Closing Techniques

Assumptive
Any question/statement that assumes that the individual has bought, agreed, accepted, et cetera.

Example:
"It appears that my background aligns really well with the role; if there are no reservations about my background, may I have the job?"

Takeaway Close
Withdraw your candidacy, interview, et cetera. You are guaranteed a "yes" or "no" 100 percent of the time.

Example:
"I get the sense that this position is no longer available or that you would not like to move forward with my candidacy. Is that correct?"

Reverse Close
Turns the buyers' reasons why they shouldn't buy into why they should. When you are faced with an objection, think of a benefit to that objection and add the phrase:

"That's the very reason you should buy!"

Example:
"That's the very reason that you should want to hire me! I would have tremendous opportunities to use my experience, organizational skills, and creativity to evaluate what you are doing right or wrong, turn it around, and add probably one of the greatest highlights to my achievement list ever!"

Elimination/Positive No Close
Ask a battery of questions to uncover unstated concerns that are inhibiting the person from making a decision. Systematically eliminate all the reasons to continue stalling. The task here is to get the hiring authority to say "yes" to you.

Example:
(You): "Well, [hiring authority], you've got to be comfortable with your decision, so let's see if we can look at it logically, okay? Tell me, are you hesitating because you do not think I can handle the duties?"
(Hiring Authority): "No, you could handle the duties just fine; in fact, you could handle them better than the other candidates."
(You): "Okay, then what about the people, do you think I would not fit in with the culture?"
(Hiring Authority): "No."
(You): [Continue asking all the questions that have been determined to be positive, and then make your last question.] "Well, that's all there is! We have covered it all! I would confidently say that you are holding back because of the universal ailment—fear of change/making a decision. It is very common. Is it fair to say that it is absolutely essential to make a logical decision so as to avoid getting caught up in an emotional one? We have just talked about all the logical reasons why I am the best candidate for the role. Let me recommend that we go ahead with a logical and intelligent decision and move ahead. Does that make sense?"

Similar Situation/Feel, Felt, Found
This close uses your past experience in making life changing decisions to help the person arrive at a decision. Do not lie.

Example:

"I know how you feel. Just last week I was interviewing with another hiring authority who felt the same way. However, they found that by meeting me in person, they were able to see how well I could handle the role . . ."

The Walking Down the Street

This close involves using an analogy. Have the person compare their current situation with an opening to the opportunity you presented by filling it.

Example:

"Imagine that you were walking down the street and you had an open position. On one side is your present company with a job not being handled. On the other side is the opportunity to hire me to fill the gap. Which side of the street would you want?"

College Professor

Helps the person to think objectively about the situation based on how a non-biased, nonemotional outsider would judge the situation.

Example:

"You are intimately and emotionally involved in this decision. Long-range employment decisions should be made, not on the basis of emotion, but on intelligent, logical reasoning. Let's say you were to ask the opinion of someone you respect, someone that has been successful: maybe a businessman, or college professor. Let's say you were to lay out all the facts about all your options and detail the experiences of the candidates, the positives and negatives, reasons for needing the position filled, all the implications, and so on. This would be someone who would take an objective view, holding nothing back. Now if you were to ask that person what their advice would be to maximize the return on investment in your hiring decisions, tell me, what advice do you think s/he would convey to you? What do you think the recommendation would be?"

Switch Places
When all else fails, ask the hiring manager to tell you what s/he would do to get the job.

Example:
"Mrs. Smith, if you were trying to get this job and you didn't know why all your efforts weren't getting you anywhere, what would you do?"

Fear of Change
Point out that fear is not a good basis for making decisions. Fear is perfectly normal but should not let it rule over someone making a rational decision.

Example:
"I understand that there is a fear in adding to staff in this type of economic climate. What is the alternative? Continue with sluggish sales performers or gaps in your territories? Is that what you want to do? There is nothing wrong with having the natural desire to stay with the things that you are comfortable with, but never let that kind of fear, the fear of leaving the comfort zone, rule your decision to improve your company and your department. I know I could make a difference."

Below are some recommendations to help you match the situation with the right style of close. After you present your case for employment, you could use whichever of these tactics seems best suited to the hiring authority and to your personal style.

If the company asks you to send your résumé, you could use:
  Assumptive
  Alternate Choice

If you get sent over to human resources, you could use:
  Reverse

Takeaway
Assumptive Close
Alternate Choice
Puppy Dog
Sharp Angle/Right Angle

If the company is uncooperative, you could use:
College Professor
Switch Place
Takeaway

If the company is hesitating on giving you an initial or follow-up interview, you could use:
Assumptive Close
Alternate Choice
Puppy Dog
Elimination Close
Ben Franklin
College Professor
Summary
Takeaway
Similar Situation
Sharp Angle/Right Angle

If you believe the company is uncertain and has a fear of change, you could use:
Elimination
Ben Franklin
College Professor
Summary
Walking Down the Street

Acknowledgments

I need to take a few words to thank those around me that have supported me during my life and have helped me to be in a position to share my experiences. The first is my wonderful partner, wife, and best friend, Amy. I actually placed her many years ago with one of my clients. I tried to hire her, but she was too expensive. I did, however, find a way for her work for me for free—I just had to marry her. It was the best placement I have ever made and through all my crazy endeavors, she is always by my side.

To my children, Megan, Jack, and Lizzie, thank you for allowing me to do what I do, even though it meant I did not spend as much time with you as I wished. But I know you understand that everything I do is for you.

I also need to take a few words to thank Alan R. Schonberg, founder of Management Recruiters International. He recruited me to move to Cleveland to help him build out the first true total human capital solutions firm in the world. He was a great friend and mentor, and without his support and guidance, I think I would never have been able to follow this path.

I also need to thank all my clients, candidates, partners, former college roommates, and associates that have supported me for over thirty-five years. My career has been about building and maintaining relationships and without their ongoing support over the years, I would never have been in a position to have and share my experiences with you.

When I first started helping people with career advice, I was always thinking about my father, Richard Johnston. During my entire life,

I saw my father demonstrate a spirit of generosity of time that I have tried to replicate for my entire life. Whenever anyone asked him for help, he always took them down to the local diner to buy them a cup of coffee and a piece of pie and would just listen and try to help. Throughout my career, I have never ignored anyone, I have always tried to find a few minutes to help. It is my deepest wish that this book can help everyone figure out a path forward. To all, keep looking for your Buffalo!

When I put this book together, it was very important to me to include other people's voices. So to all of those listed below, thank you so much for your time and contributions; it means a lot to me and I am sure all my readers will appreciate your thoughtful suggestions and advice.

Thank You:

- Howard L. Lewis
- Peter Quigley
- Brandon Chrostowski
- Robin Toft
- Abid Hamid
- Gary Buckland
- Elizabeth Johnston
- Bob Weiler
- Allan Hartley
- Dennis Kozlowski
- William Kubicek
- Kennon Kincaid
- Kevin Anderson
- Treva Offutt